COACHING in CONTEXT

HELPING OTHERS REACH HIGHER

DR. WIL CHEVALIER

WESTBOW
PRESS®
A DIVISION OF THOMAS NELSON
& ZONDERVAN

WestBow Press books may be ordered through booksellers or by contacting:

WestBow Press
A Division of Thomas Nelson & Zondervan
1663 Liberty Drive
Bloomington, IN 47403
www.westbowpress.com
1 (866) 928-1240

ISBN: 978-1-9736-7544-0 (sc)
ISBN: 978-1-9736-8473-2 (hc)
ISBN: 978-1-9736-7543-3 (e)

Print information available on the last page.

WestBow Press rev. date: 01/29/2020

Contents

Acknowledgments

Special thanks and my deepest gratitude to: Alyssa Carr, Bonnie Kyle, Jeanette Morris, Susan Titus Osborn, and Bill Heatley for their outstanding editorial assistance.

In addition, I would like to acknowledge the insightful input from Rev. Teko and Gabrielle Bailey, Ruth Co, Gary Coffey, Rev. Jim Folkers, Darlene Hoffa, Gary Haas, Dr. Sandra Hardy, Ron Kelleher, Rick Leavenworth, Tony Kitt, Bob Sigler, and Paul Stevens.

Endorsements from Around the World

BOLIVIA

Coaching in Context is a powerful manual for those who want to train others or transmit a Christian lifestyle. It also might be used by parents with their kids, or to apply to their own life. This manuscript came into my hands at just the right moment during a time of decisions in my ministry. I needed to take a moment to review my personal goals, so it became a great resource for me. I have no doubt anyone can use it for personal growth. It is highly recommended. **Marco A. Saavedra, Professor in Theology, Chairman Board of Directors of Centro de Vida, Santa Cruz**

CUBA

True leadership is an odd specimen, and fostering positive patterns can be a challenge for those who see the need but fail to meet it. With *Coaching in Context*, Wil Chevalier gives us an eye-opening tool that teaches us what real coaching is about, and also helps us touch it with our own hands. On the ground of the mentee's context, Dr. Chevalier starts building from the very foundation—our relationship with our Creator—and keeps adding from the blueprint, the Bible. I recommend this manual to those want to grow and help others grow into the image of the model of unsurpassable excellence in coaching, Jesus. **David Gomero Borges, Nakar Translations, Baracoa, Guantánamo, Cuba**

HAITI

Dr. Chevalier's extensive cross-cultural immersions have equipped him to understand people and their cultures at a level far deeper than what can be observed with the naked eye. Readers will benefit from his wealth of experience and wisdom. Yet, what makes *Coaching in Context* an invaluable resource is that it is an invitation to all aspiring and practicing coaches to let the Holy Spirit coach us first, guiding us through the timeless truths of the Bible about helping others achieve their goals. Anyone who reads and applies the principles Dr. Chevalier lays down will not only become an effective and successful coach, but also a spiritually mature individual. **Rev. Dr. Guenson Charlot, Professor of Biblical Preaching and Theology at Emmaus University, Cap Haitien**

INDIA

Coaching in Context is an impeccable tool for leaders who desire to grow by investing equitable time and energies into their mentees for favorable outcomes. The book precisely dissects practical aspects of mentorship and coaching based on biblical principles and exudes the immense experience of Dr. Wil Chevalier on coaching others. It teaches how to actively oversee the holistic transformation of future leaders with godly love and humility for a greater cause. I sincerely feel that the readers of this book will be able to save themselves from the pain, stress, and displaced relationships that come with leading and mentoring others if not done right. **Rev. Vineet Joy Massey, Co-Founder, The Foundation Church, New Delhi**

MYANMAR

Good leaders learn from leaders and beget leaders. *Coaching in Context* is informative about the "what," "why," "how" of coaching. No one is too old or too young to coach someone as long as he or she can listen attentively, ask the right questions, maintain the trust level, and be accountable. Dr. Wil Chevalier is a great mentor for marriage and family, and his book has given me so many valuable insights for my leadership journey. I strongly recommend *Coaching in Context* to fellow pastors and leaders who have the heart to raise up servant leaders for our world today! **Rev. Dr. John Tuan Hre Thang, Every Nation Church Yangon, Yangon**

PHILIPPINES

Coaching in Context reflects a lot of Wil Chevalier's personal journey in loving people by mentoring and coaching them. I came to understand the value of coming alongside people, caring for them enough to lovingly assist them toward real personal growth and development through Wil's discipleship ministry. This is an excellent manual with strong biblical support and lots of practical tools to assist you in all kinds of mentoring/coaching contexts. **Rev. Enrico J. Dizon, Pastor for Growth—Greenhills Christian Fellowship, Metro Manila**

Coaching in Context is simple, doable, practical, and biblical. In it, Dr. Chevalier teaches the "What?" and trains on the "How?" He guides his reader through the contextual process of precepts-principles-practicals. From somebody who has grown to good health in relationships through the able and doable counselling and coaching of Dr. Wil Chevalier, which I now replicate in my own marriage and family ministry, I humbly recommend *Coaching in Context*. **Rev. Arnold G. Perona, Pastor, Marriage Mentor—Greenhills Christian Fellowship**

During a conversation (in 2018), with Senator Manny Pacquiao (see Back cover endorsement) I asked, "…when it comes to your personal family life, do you have any tips or insights you would like to communicate regarding real 'success'? I'd like to share your ideas with the pastors I'm coaching later tonight." Now, Manny Pacquiao was born in poverty, so he knows what it's like to go to school without sleep and endure a day without food. And, typically, of the soft-spoken senator with a burning passion for Christ, his response was, "Unfortunately things can happen to pastors when they become well known and famous. I would say, 'Don't let it all go to your head. Regardless of the fame and all, don't stop being a light for Jesus…"

Perhaps this is why Philippians 4:12 is one of his favorite verses in the Bible: "I know what it is to be in need, and I know what it is to have plenty. I have learned the secret of being content in any and every situation, whether well fed or hungry, whether living in plenty or in want."

SOUTH AFRICA

In *Coaching in Context,* Dr. Wil Chevalier shows us the basic imperative of Christian discipleship that honors God. This book should be an essential tool for leaders of all spheres who know Jesus as their Lord and Saviour to assist them to seek and invest in knowing the context of any one individual whom God puts in their way to coach. Dr. Wil calls us to a deeper, costly relational search of a person's history and present before we can offer conclusive guidance about what they need to do and become. I am more than happy to commend the book, which is a direct reflection of the author's character and the God he serves. **Rev. Elvis Mvulane, Pastor/National Director, WALK THROUGH THE BIBLE**

UNITED KINGDOM

Coaching in Context is a timely and effective manual for the church at large, especially in today's uncertain world. Governments, businesses, and even churches have difficulties navigating the future. People tend to live day-by-day, abating risks and unexpected events. Dr. Wil Chevalier has invigorated the ministry of coaching—a vital Christian service desperately needed in today's society. I sincerely endorse this well-thought-out manual to people whom God will call to help others navigate their own walks of life. **Rev. Rene R. Nepomuceno, International Director, Word International Ministries (WIN)**

UNITED STATES

Coaching in Context is an excellent tool for pastors. Having spent a large part of my life in pastoral ministry, I very often found myself seeking to accomplish the very thing this book so adequately discusses. I would encourage anyone in any phase of ministry to give strong attention to the wisdom Dr. Chevalier so effectively lays out in this book. Having watched his life for many years, I can strongly affirm that he is a man of integrity who practices what he preaches...or writes about. **Dr. Donald Shoff, Church Planter Director, Fellowship of Evangelical Pastors**

Coaching in Context is an excellent manual on how transformation really happens. It spells out in clear detail how God works in the life of an individual, restoring and transforming through relationship with Him and others. It also gives practical tools for those wanting to know more about how to coach another person through question-asking, accountability, and proper understanding of background and context. This is a great resource for anyone trying to help individuals in the area of personal growth and development. **Dr. Mary Simms, Therapist, Author**

If you are a pastor, a pastoral trainer, a mentor, or a personal/life coach, you will find Dr. Chevalier's Coaching in Context to be a valuable guide for a more fulfilling and God-honoring ministry. **Nick Vujicic, Australian Christian evangelist and motivational speaker**

Introduction

What Is Coaching in Context?

Coaching in Context is a valuable resource for anyone working in Christian leadership development, coaching, mentoring, and discipleship that will expand and enhance your God-honoring ministry with wisdom and practical lessons about the dynamics of effective coaching.

Context is a crucial factor for both the coach and the person being coached. Context informs the process of growth by asking insightful and relevant questions. As my friend Ravi Zacharias puts it, "Behind every question is a questioner, and behind every questioner is a network of assumptions, hurts, struggles, and often prejudices."

Context is vital for developing, promoting, and nurturing relationships that are based on trust and are the basis for asking thoughtful and insightful questions. Trust is vital, and the coach must ensure that optimal levels of trust exist between coach and trainee. The combination of trust and mutually understood context will ensure that the results of coaching questions will be focused and amplified.

Coaching, Mentoring, and Discipleship

Throughout the Gospels, Jesus used all three of these teaching methods. In Luke 9:2, Jesus sends His disciples out "to proclaim the kingdom of God and to heal." He does this after he has modeled those actions in Luke 8. Jesus involved the disciples in ministry that

He easily could have accomplished Himself—just as a parent teaches a child. On their return from this assignment, Jesus drew the disciples together to reflect on their experiences, allowing them an opportunity for timely, specific feedback—a powerful teaching tool. And He took advantage of teachable moments. Instead of pronouncing a sermon in the middle of the situation with hard-hearted Samaritans, he stopped to model humility (See Luke 9:51-56).

Many people associate coaching with athletics, where the desired result is increased success in a specific sport. However, coaching can also mean helping someone do what is necessary to accomplish a desired goal. Coaches train and instruct others, and their goal is to improve the performance of the person being coached. The concept of the word "coach" indicates "a private tutor." And while many people use the terms "coaching" and "mentoring" interchangeably, they are two different approaches to assisting others in personal transformation and development.

Discipleship is another term we often use in connection with coaching and mentoring, but it has its own unique function in bringing about change in a person's life. Each approach has a place and value, but it is helpful to understand the distinctions.

Coaching: is *drawing out from someone what God has put inside and helping to mold and shape it into a beneficial and effective form.* Coaches listen more than they talk, ask questions that allow a person to discover and recognize his or her own goals, helping in establishing the necessary network of support, encouragement, and accountability for the goals to be realized.

Suppose a pastor wanted to be a better Christian leader. He might seek out the help of a coach and become their trainee. The coach might ask them these questions:

- How do you see yourself fulfilling your calling as a Christian?
- What opportunities for growth and learning currently exist for you?

- How do you define success for yourself and how will you know you are successful?
- Describe your strengths and development needs as an effective leader and team member.

With this context in mind the coach would begin to:

- Work with the pastor to find specific areas of growth and explore means of growth.
- Help improve their development needs in working as a team player with others.
- Help them set goals to track their progress, etc.

Mentoring: can be defined as *imparting to another what God has done in your life.* A mentee seeks to learn from an older or more experienced person (the mentor). Similar to discipleship, mentoring also involves mentees gleaning wisdom and practical advice from a mentor. For example, a woman who has successfully reared her own children might mentor a younger mom with small children, providing encouragement, support, and experience. Often mentors meet one-on-one with their mentees, sharing specific life lessons and examples of the way God has guided or directed them through various circumstances or difficulties.

Discipleship: a disciple is *a pupil, apprentice, or adherent to the life and teachings of another,* and discipleship is the process by which those who are devoted to a respected teacher follow his or her teaching. The English word *disciple* (in Greek, *mathetes*), means "to learn." The goal of the *mathetes* (learner) is to become like the teacher. A new believer, for instance, benefits from a relationship in which he or she is introduced to basic information and instruction about how to build a solid relationship with God. The new believer might learn the importance of serving family or community, setting aside time for worship, prayer, and Bible reading (a guided curriculum, etc.), while observing the teacher modeling these practices in healthy ways.

Coaches, mentors, and disciplers act as change-agents, helping a person move from where they are (taking off the old self) to where they want to be (putting on the new). In practical terms, the person being coached (the trainee) does most of the talking. They are responding to perceptive questions from the coach that are carefully constructed to assist with the development of personal goals. By comparison, mentoring or discipleship sessions typically have the mentor or teacher doing most of the talking as they impart skills, information, and personal experiences deemed helpful to the growth of the mentee or disciple.

Again, coaching, mentoring, and discipleship are all important forms of transformation in spiritual and personal development and they frequently overlap one another. This manual will focus primarily on the principles and aims of coaching. As you work with an individual, you will find there are times when providing significant input is appropriate. At other times, you will help individuals make their own discoveries and set their own goals in response to your questions, which I have found to be more beneficial. Every once in a while, someone simply needs to be encouraged, signaling a moment for you to be a mentor and share about how God has brought about victory in your own life.

Why Coaching Is Different

Even though people have the right to believe "anything" they choose, that does not mean that "anything" a person believes is right. Similarly, transformation is not a byproduct of receiving information; transformation is relational. For instance, knowing all *about* what's inside the Bible won't change any of us. Neither will "knowing" other Christians, talking with them at church, or listening to sermons.

Transformation requires being responsive to the Holy Spirit's direction. It means wholeheartedly living out God's Word by following the example and life of Jesus. It requires walking with other believers in sincerity, humility, and truth. It calls for Christians walking side-by-side, helping one another grow through example, encouragement, and rebuke. Coaching is a developmental approach that seeks to take these realities seriously. In my work with leaders, I have come to greatly appreciate one-liners that go something like this one: *"We need to seek criticism from those who do not want to criticize us, while not getting sidetracked by those who do."*

As a coach, if you want great feedback, you must seek it out. Why seek out criticism? Because if you want *constructive feedback*, you cannot just expect it to happen—you must seek it (Matthew 6:33). Before publishing this book, for example, I asked several qualified people to answer these questions: "Can this manuscript be improved somehow?" and "If you were to make changes, how would you change it?" On the other hand, you will also be wise not to be sidetracked by those who only want to offer criticism just to tear you down. So, seek constructive feedback from qualified people who will address the issue at hand by targeting specific areas that need improvement.

This is the same advice given by Dr. John Townsend who has been helping millions of people change their lives for more than three decades:

> You need perceptive people who can help you look at your blind spots. You need feedback and information from others who understand the growth paths, so that you don't take more wrong turns than you need to. And you need others who understand and identify with what growing and leadership are all about since leadership and growth require someone who 'gets it.' So make sure that whatever you engage in on a growth level involves safe, accepting, honest, and competent people: the kind of people you can trust and who are like the person you want to become as well. (Dr. John Townsend, *Leadership Beyond Reason*)

We can seek to imitate Christ's work and life by applying His methods, but at the end of the day, God is the only one able to bring about growth in a person's life. Such change is fostered through our willingness to be transformed, the work of the Holy Spirit, application of biblical principles, and involvement in a fellowship of believers—the Church. *Coaching in Context* is an approach that attempts to help you take all of these factors into account.

What You Will Learn

In order to attain maximum effectiveness in our Coaching Bootcamps, I have found it profitable for the participants to see coaching demonstrated, experience coaching themselves, and then have them practice their coaching skills on others. Some of the groups who have used this material include pastors and church leaders who have sought coaching for themselves, or those who wanted to know more about how to coach themselves. Some of these leaders wanted to teach coaching to small groups or even whole congregations.

This manual is designed to prepare you, in your role as coach, for the challenges of daily life by emphasizing spiritual growth and transformation—for yourself first and then your trainee—through your coaching relationship. Various tools and suggestions are presented to help you get closer to this goal. It is my hope that you will come away from *Coaching in Context* with a greater understanding of your own needs, your trainee's needs, and how to practically meet those needs in a coaching session. You will be given tools to communicate, plan, and grow personally and then share with your trainee. So, as you coach others on the road to success, be aware of the qualities to look for in those you pour your heart into.

"And what you have heard from me in the presence of many witnesses entrust to faithful men, who will be able to teach others also" (2 Timothy 2:2 ESV).

The first chapter deals with your relationship and connection to God. Who is Jesus and what has He done for us? What is the Holy Spirit's role in your life? What help does the Bible provide? What is the role of repentance? In chapter two, you will find tools for managing your own health and growth while coaching others in need. The third chapter contains information about building a relationship with the person you are coaching that involves humility, creativity, and transparency. In chapter four, we examine the power of prayer and how crucial prayer is to the acceptance of responsibility for another person's spiritual journey. You will be encouraged to trust God to guide your coaching choices and decisions by asking Him to show you the best steps forward in the power of the Holy Spirit.

The final four sections of this manual include tips for achieving constructive communication, crafting reasonable plans and expectations, and maintaining a constant attitude of growth and progress. Finally, the appendices provide practical materials and information to aid the process of self-reflection, goal completion, and the assessment of spiritual skills and gifts.

Goals, structure, timing, topics, etc. of your coaching can vary, but the best thing to do after reading this book is to practice and refine what you've learned with the individuals you are coaching.

A Journey with Jesus

Ultimately, as a coach, you're using your influence to encourage those you coach to do the right thing and inspiring them to do their best. Your role is not to get those you coach to *do things* but to *inspire them* to establish positive habits and patterns that will help them reach the finish line in ways that honor God. You are helping people see that Jesus has an important context in their own lives. *Coaching in Context* focuses on encouraging the person you're coaching to draw on the power of the Holy Spirit in order to accomplish what they seek to achieve. Most importantly, coaching in context is not something we do *for* God, but *with* God.

CHAPTER 1

Knowing God

Coaching is the art of leading an individual to a goal, a level of performance, a direction, or a virtue that he or she desires to achieve. It is important to know that coaches can have a powerful effect on a person's life. As believers—with our foundation inherently rooted in our relationship with God—we hold without question that *transformation* requires a *personal* relationship with God: "Visionary Christian leaders have made it plain that you cannot know God's vision for your ministry unless you first know God" (George Barna, *The Power of Vision*).

Moreover, our idea of who God is invariably affects our personal priorities and determines what we will do and why (James 1:22). We should remember that our identity is rooted in Christ, so we do not let accomplishing goals become a barometer for measuring our self-worth. A focus on accomplishing causes *success* to lead us to pride and arrogance, while *failure to reach your goals* will lead to despair. Again, your identity is rooted in Christ—not in your accomplishments in life. As Dallas Willard often said, "What matters is not the accomplishments you achieve; what matters is the person you become."

Foundational to a successful coaching-in-context experience is a deep understanding of God's love and grace toward us in Christ, access to Him through His Spirit, and God's revelation to us in His Word. With these truths as the core of our efforts, we can more sensitively pursue assessing the spiritual condition of the trainee and point him or her toward the fullness of life that God has planned.

Understanding Grace: Jesus Is More than a Role Model

Most struggles experienced in life are the result of the human condition. No one is free from the effects of the fall of Adam and Eve in the garden. *"For all have sinned and fall short of the glory of God"* (Romans 3:23 NIV).

From time immemorial, humanity has struggled with how to deal with sin and its consequences. The human answer to the problem of sin has always been to cover shame (Genesis 3:7) and hide from guilt (Genesis 3:8). Due to the problem of original sin, these bad habits of the heart remain alive in our behavior, often with profound effects. Sometimes even well-meaning attempts to show us our sin and ongoing need for Christ only move us to cover shame and guilt with good works done in the flesh. When this happens, "Christianity" simply becomes a set of principles that people struggle to follow, trying to earn their way into God's favor with self-denial and obedience.

Stuck in this destructive legalism, it is easy to be drawn toward moral self-help programs and subconscious attempts to please God by modeling Christ's character apart from openness to the Cross and the Spirit (Galatians 3:1-3). Human efforts in the power of the flesh simply provide a subtle, and often unconscious, way to appease conscience and cover the true state of the heart, creating a deeper form of self-deception.

In the end, a person's justification and acceptance by faith are the only cures for guilt before God. Because of Christ's obedience on the cross, God no longer condemns those who believe in Jesus

(Romans 5:9; 8:1; 2 Corinthians 5:21). Any awareness of sin and failure should instead become a door to confession that leads to honest self-awareness and deeper dependence on God and *His grace*. There are several methods of confession/repentance and the trainee's context should inform the coach how to help facilitate this important process.

Confession allows us to be open and honest as we come out of hiding from our sin and honestly see ourselves in the light of God's grace and constant acceptance, because the gifts of faith and obedience that we offer Him were purchased with His blood.

Christian maturity is a long, slow process involving a life of obedience, love, and joy before God. Knowing that we cannot fix ourselves, we must go to something—Someone—better, Jesus Christ. Only Christ can atone for sin and allow us to work out our salvation by relentlessly grounding our human efforts in His finished work of dealing with sin on the cross. As the apostle Paul declared among the idols of Mars Hill: *"The God who made the world and everything in it is the Lord of heaven and earth and does not live in temples built by hands. And He is not served by human hands, as if he needed anything. Rather, He himself gives everyone life and breath and everything else"* (Acts 17:24-25 NIV).

Everything we have is given to us by God Himself, *"It is because of Him that you are in Christ Jesus, who has become for us wisdom from God—that is, our righteousness, holiness, and redemption. Therefore, as it is written: 'Let the one who boasts boast in the Lord'"* (1 Corinthians 1:30-31).

The Holy Spirit's Transforming Work

Experienced coaches are acquainted with walking people through various life transitions and changes. As such, Christian coaching involves helping the people they coach to grow in their love for God and their service to people. The process involves encouraging men and women who know Him to become more sensitive to the leading of His Holy Spirit as we coach. Christian issues might not appear frequently in conversations with non-Christian clients, yet coaches are very much aware of the need to have God at the center of their coaching. The coaching sessions allow the Holy Spirit to work in the client, rather than having the coach bring an agenda. Therefore, *coaching in context* is about helping a person explore, develop, and then live out a more intimate relationship with God.

Experienced coaches realize that they cannot take someone on a journey they haven't yet travelled. A coach's transformation, experience, openness, and obedience to the Holy Spirit is the value they bring to coaching. Only then can they use that skill to assist their trainee. It takes a lifetime for people, coach or trainee, to develop more and more Christ-like character. This Christlikeness is what allows the coach to train someone else how to open his or her heart to the transforming work of the Holy Spirit. The coach's relationship with the Holy Spirit, focused on transformation through relationship and accountability, will provide a model for the trainee and prepare them how to coach others.

The Role of Repentance

In this book, we will be focusing on positive transformation in our life and in the life of our trainee. Before anyone can begin living a new life, they must first let go of the old one. The biblical terms for this concept are repentance and self-denial. Coaching, mentoring, and discipling all rely on this important truth. Repentance simply means realizing that your life is going in the wrong direction, that you are not the person you should be, and deciding to turn and follow Jesus. The gospel of Jesus is rooted in this idea of repentance:

"The time is fulfilled, and the kingdom of God has come near; **repent**, *and believe in the good news."* (Mark 1:15 NRSV)

Once we have turned (repented) and are pointed in the right

direction, we can begin to engage in transformative actions and ways of living that are aided by God's grace. Paul calls this process stripping off the old self and putting on the new self (Colossians 3:9-10). Jesus calls this process self-denial or death-to-self where the old lesser self is "crucified" and the "life from above" becomes more and more a part of who you are through the resurrection power of Christ (Matthew 10:38-39, Mark 8:34-38, Luke 9:23). Remember that transformation requires both a turning and a self-denial, because the old life of the flesh is at odds with the new life in the Spirit.

Live by the Spirit, I say, and do not gratify the desires of the flesh. For what the flesh desires is opposed to the Spirit, and what the Spirit desires is opposed to the flesh; for these are opposed to each other, to prevent you from doing what you want. (Galatians 5:16-17 NRSV)

Whenever you are working on change and transformation, in yourself or your trainee, remember that it involves the two processes of turning and self-denial.

Understanding God's Word: The Living Road Map for Transformation

The Word of God is alive and brings us into alignment with the purpose our Father designed us for even before our conception.

We were created to know the mind of God and let that mind dwell in us. From God's revelation in His Word, we come to understand how we should live (Ezekiel 33:10; Psalm 119:105). In this context, we recognize Jesus Christ as the one from whom all definitions for living with purpose are drawn.

The Bible helps us chart a godly course by providing a foundation for daily living in this world. Biblical commands give us unwavering anchors for behavior (Matthew 22:34-40, 28:20). The Bible is our blueprint for living and should be every Christian coach's manual. Scripture is clear about God's desire to set people free, forgive them of their sins, and restore their lives. And in our relationship with

Christ, we find true freedom—freedom from fear, freedom from the domination of our genetic weaknesses, and freedom from the control of others. Zig Zigler sums it up well when he quips: "Fear is the darkroom where negatives are developed."

It is imperative that we, and those we coach, be exposed to the truth of God's Word (Joshua 1:8). By internalizing the Bible, which is a living, breathing source of wisdom, we find guidance for knowing what to embrace and what to avoid (Psalm 119:11). This requires a lifelong commitment to learning and allowing the Holy Spirit to influence and challenge us. This is the Word that allows us to reason together with God and with each other. *"If you abide in Me, and My words abide in you, ask whatever you wish, and it will be done for you"* (John 15:7).

As a Christian leader, whatever your skill level of "coaching," it is well to remember that you are an ordinary person. Therefore, it should come as no surprise that there might be discomforting times when God's presence may "feel" obscure to you. Though the evidence from God's Word assures us of His presence—that He is there based on what the Bible tells us—we can still have feelings of doubt. This is when we need to remind ourselves *by His unfailing Word* that God is near (Hebrews 13:5-6). When the assurance of His presence is based on our "feelings," the promises of God Word might remain out of reach.

In his powerful book about the bombing raids of World War II, *Sleeping with Bread,* Dennis Linn tells the story of thousands of children orphaned and left to starve. After experiencing being abandoned, many of them were rescued and sent to refugee camps. Many of them were terrified and could not sleep at night, despite the good care they received. They thought they would awake to find themselves homeless and hungry once again. Nothing the caregivers did seemed to help, until someone thought to send a child to bed with a loaf of bread. Holding their bread, the children were able to sleep. If they woke up frightened in the night, the bread seemed to remind them, "I ate today, and I will eat again tomorrow." When God's words abide in us, we are reminded, like the frightened orphaned children in this story, that our Father will never forsake us.

The Bible as Our Lens: Coaching from a Biblical Worldview

As a coach, you are using your training and experience to help individuals look at life situations from multiple viewpoints. As such, it is imperative to remember that a biblical worldview is the ultimate lens through which we see everything else. Why? Because God's Word is the clearest means that God has chosen to communicate truth, healing, and salvation (Psalm 107:20).

Moreover, everyone has a worldview. Having a worldview is unavoidable, as Dallas Willard puts it in *Knowing Christ Today*:

> Whenever we act, we act with reference to a 'world,' a totality of facts, goods, and possibilities. A worldview is, therefore, a biological necessity for human beings, because we act, whether consciously or not, with reference to a whole (a 'world'). Our 'view' of that whole determines what we shall undertake to deal with or omit in our actions day-by-day and hour-by-hour. It dictates what we will or will not count on as resources and recognize as dangers. It determines our aims and our means and, eventually the quality of our life and the kind of person we will become.

More consequences, on every matter of value and relationship, follow from one's belief or disbelief in God than from any other issue. A longtime friend, Ron Jensen, says in *Make a Life, Not Just a Living*:

> Just as there are physical laws that govern the physical universe, so there are universal principles that govern

our existence. These are laws that, if violated, have inevitable repercussions in our lives. These principles are abiding truths—universal, absolute, nonnegotiable. They are as factual as the law of gravity. We may not understand them, or buy into them, but that doesn't invalidate them. They simply won't move; they are firm. Our choice is either to discover and fully embrace them and thereby succeed as we are meant to, or to ignore them and fail without ever knowing why.

Just as medicine, education, and other disciplines can be used to help people heal and grow, scientific research and insights from psychology can contribute to the resource toolbox for the Christian coach. The Word of God, however, is foundational; it is the ultimate authority on life and behavior. It is crucial in helping people gain perspective by stepping back and looking at the bigger picture of God's Word. Consider some of these distinctives of coaching from a biblical perspective:

Goals: In general, coaches seek to find solutions to emotional, attitudinal, and perceptional problems. They encourage, strengthen, and support those who are discouraged and lack confidence, among other issues. But the Christian coach goes further, by drawing out unique, *spiritual* goals like encouraging repentance and self-denial through the confession of sin and seeking forgiveness when necessary. The coach helps the person being coached to live out their faith in practical everyday life and to fellowship and worship with other Christians.

Methods: A Christian coach whose lens is the Bible will not use any method to help, assist, gain information, or advise that is inconsistent with Scripture. Sessions are likely to include praying, confronting, and reading Scripture (2 Timothy 3:16-17).

Coach: The internal character of the Christian coach is as important as the goals and methods they may use (Matthew 7:5). Ideally, coaches model Jesus Christ, the "Wonderful Counselor," and how He cared for and counseled people. In articulating the caring component of the coach, Ron Jensen in *Make a Life, Not Just a Living* writes: "People are encouraged when they see growth in themselves. But growth doesn't just happen. It is ignited and fanned by caring people around us who help us develop a skill, adjust an attitude, build a mental framework, and gain an insight."

Like Jesus, a coach will demonstrate compassion, sensitivity, commitment to the Father and to prayer, a deep love and personal knowledge of Scripture, and encouragement to an individual to grow in Christ in dependence on the Holy Spirit.

Chapter 2

Knowing Yourself

Focusing on knowing God is a critical first step in learning how to coach in context. Each of us has a different context, and we come to a personal relationship with God on our own terms. Some people grow up as atheists. Others grow up in the Church. Our backgrounds may vary, but our relationship with God is an individual one.

In this chapter, we shift our focus to your own self-awareness. How well do you know you? Before you begin coaching and attempting to help others discover more about themselves, it is important that you know yourself and your own context.

Biographical Reflection and Assessment

How do you get to know *you*? You look in the mirror in the morning and see ... you. You fix or comb your hair, and you may adjust your collar or shirt. But how do others see you? How does your personality come across to others?

God created you to be a unique individual, designed to be an integral part of His family. Understanding how He made you, how He has used and will use you, and what His purposes are for your life are essential elements of the coaching process.

You begin this process of knowing yourself by reflecting on your life in many different areas. Perhaps success and high achievement were common in your upbringing. On the other hand, seeing failure and disappointment in yourself may be a consistent pattern. For most of us, life has brought a combination of outcomes that we consider both good and bad. Loss is a part of life, and I have found Dr. John Townsend's insights in *Leadership Beyond Reason* in dealing with failure, disappointments, and losses to be very helpful. He writes, "Losses have three sources: you, others, and the world. Your own failures and lapses in judgment can cause a loss. Others in your life can be the source. And sometimes, the economy, the weather, or illness that is no one's fault can cause it. More often than not, the losses you experience are some combination of the three. But remember that as a leader, you will lose."

To begin your career in coaching, you will need to make a personal assessment. You probably already have a general idea of what you are about. However, utilizing assessment tools with focused areas of personal behavior will help you see yourself. I've included a survey for you to complete in Appendix A: Biographical Reflection and Assessment.

A good coach will trust that God is at work, especially in hard times or bad situations, and willingly abandon the final outcomes to God. Reviewing how God has worked through your successes and victories along with your frustrations and regrets will bring insight into how He wants to use you in the future. Your victory over those difficult times brings solid spiritual growth and results in life messages that God can use powerfully in the lives of others. Ask God to show you how He has used all kinds of experiences in shaping your life to bring about growth and spiritual maturity.

Take a moment right now to complete this assessment, and take a few moments to journal about your reflection:

1. What have you concluded?
2. What are the major things happening in your life right now?
3. How would you like your life to be different one year from now?

Accelerating Personal Growth

Can we change on our own? The short answer is yes. But if done alone, growth and transformation is a slow and painful process. Indeed, it may take a lifetime. As Christians, we have help. When we put our lives into the hands of Jesus, everything changes.

Jesus took twelve men—a mix from various walks of life—and made them His disciples. Over the course of three years, Jesus transformed their lives in such a powerful way that they would later begin the transformation of the entire world. What is their legacy? We now have over a billion Christians living in the world today.

Jesus instructed His disciples to make disciples of all nations, teaching them to obey everything He had commanded them. (See Matthew 28:19-20.) He sent them out to be His witnesses in their own nation, in neighboring cultures, and to the most remote parts of the earth, announcing the message of salvation by grace through faith. Development of Christian leadership can have a profound impact on completing this enormous task. This is why it is important to put a high value on our own personal growth. Every minute invested in this effort is time well spent, and Jesus will use, transform, and bless whatever we give to Him. "Yesterday is a canceled check; tomorrow is a promissory note; today is the only cash you have—so spend it wisely" (Kay Lyons).

Doing the Clifton's StrengthsFinder assessment test at www. gallups.com/strengthsfinder could also help you better understand your natural strengths and how you're wired to think, as well as help you become more aware of your tendencies. There are thirty-four strengths that each person has naturally. However, your top five strengths are the most dominant. Taking the time to understand your natural strengths and how you use them on a daily basis in making decisions can help accelerate your growth as a coach as well as help you focus more on the things that are a better fit for you. Knowing and understanding your strengths can have a tremendous impact on your Christian walk and how you influence others.

Recognizing Stress Triggers

Have you ever seen someone overreact to something said in a way that was totally out of character? The calm, peaceful, and wise person you are at work may not be same person you are when you have to deal with your noisy neighbor or a not-so-nice mother-in-law. We may say they're being overly emotional. Emotional triggers are people, words, opinions, or situations that tend to provoke an intense and excessive emotional reaction within us. Common emotions that we experience while being triggered include anger, sadness, and fear. And we all have areas of our lives that are triggered when we're under too much stress. Yet, in most cases, how we see our self is not the way we respond when someone touches one of our "trigger buttons."

The U.S. Marine Corp does not confer the title of "Marine" on a recruit until each trainee has endured thirteen weeks of extreme physical training, culminating with the Crucible: fifty-four hours of physical and mental hardship and stress, as well as food and sleep deprivation. In this way, they stretch the Marine's tolerance under stress and prepare him or her for battle.

Until we have navigated our own stress-producing processes in life, we will be subject to triggers that pull on our emotional abilities. Reflecting on the following questions can help us to measure our effort, *not our results,* and help us become more aware of ourselves.

-For Contemplation-

What areas in life cause you stress?

What have you done to help manage your stress levels?

How can you stretch your emotional abilities?

When the mind is expected to process something overwhelming, it can succumb to stress and react in unusual and dramatic ways. Physical effects are evident when we lose sleep and our appetite. This leads quickly into emotional distress, anxiety, and fear. If we are not careful, we will isolate ourselves from loved ones who care about us. Some of these themes will be discussed, and can be applied more fully to coaching, in Marshall Goldsmith's book, *Triggers*, where he examines the environmental and psychological triggers that can derail us at work and in life.

It is well to remember that when we're fatigued and confused, we often withdraw from others and the Lord. However, there are ways to overcome these trigger points and develop meaningful change. One effective way is to remember God's call to *"cease striving and know that I am God... And the peace of God, which surpasses all comprehension, will guard your hearts and minds in Jesus Christ"* (Psalm 46:10; Philippians 4:7).

Balancing Ministry and Family

Balance. This is a term we hear frequently when it comes to work and social life. How do you balance your life now? How well do you know your ability to balance life? Are you prone to take on too many projects? Is it difficult for you to say no?

As a coach, it will be important to you and your family to balance ministry and calling with your family in a healthy way. Being a coach requires finding a healthy balance between them. This is not always an easy task. We are to be good leaders of our family, and we are responsible for our coaching relationships, imitating the example of Christ's ministry of caring for others. The apostle Paul encouraged us twice to *"not become weary in doing good"* (Galatians 6:9; 2 Thessalonians 3:13). Surely this means that having a family and doing God's work should never be a heavy burden. Too often, we grab for an intervention approach after our home plunges into chaos. Think about it this way: Our bodies are made up of many different systems (circulatory, digestive, respiratory, etc.), and we think in terms of *health* when these systems are in balance. Whenever these bodily systems are out of balance, we think in terms of *disease.*

In like manner, think about the overlap in *ministry* (or work) and *family* as the integration of the sub-systems all working together as one entire system—promoting your overall health: spiritual, emotional, psychological, relational, financial, etc. With Christ at the core (heart) of the entire system, we are continually receiving and drawing upon God's grace, which spills out into all relationships with other people throughout the day. When you are spiritually healthy, the other spheres will fall into their proper place. Christ must be Lord of all.

Therefore, we need a *preventative* approach to keep our family relationships healthy and satisfying. We can begin by looking at our family as a precious gift rather than a burden we have to handle before getting to the "real stuff" of serving God. Therefore, be cautious regarding compassion fatigue (a.k.a. burnout) by considering the following suggestions:

1. Taking time to rest is not optional; it is a necessity for growth, maturity, and health. We have a calling to show care and compassion to hurting people. Nonetheless, we must be very cautious that we do not allow our labor in the name of God to put our marriage, family, and other significant relationships in peril. (See Ephesians 5:25; 6:4.) We need blocks of time on a regular basis to rest our bodies and recharge our souls.

2. The cost of caring is high because it is often difficult to admit that we could ever run out of energy to care for our family, or to help people fulfill God's will. God's Word suggests we try this: *"As each one has received a special gift, employ it in serving one another as good stewards of the manifold grace of God ...*

whoever serves is to do so as one who is serving by the strength which God supplies" (1 Peter 4:10-11b).

3. Be mindful of the amount of suffering and emotional upheaval you're absorbing. Remember that we are total beings and that God never intended for His people to be overwhelmed by the circumstances of their family or their ministry. *"When my anxious thoughts multiply within me, Your consolations delight my soul"* (Psalm 94:19). Be aware that there is also the danger of allowing images and conversations to intrude into your mind by internalizing the suffering of others, which can lead you into *compassion fatigue, or ministry burnout.* What if you made the choice to spend an evening with your family rather than take on one more responsibility at church?

4. Take steps to promote self-care. We must learn to nourish the various parts of our total being—not just the spiritual component—because we are thinkers and feelers as well as physical and relational beings. (See Ecclesiastes 5:18-20.)

5. We must learn to be responsible stewards of our time and remember to eat, sleep, rest, and exercise properly.

    a. Schedule time for breaks and stick to the schedule. (See Mark 6:31.)
    b. Plan for laughter. Allowing laughter in our lives on a regular basis helps us achieve balance. (See Proverbs 17:22.)
    c. Strive to be good caretakers of our own health if we want to be more productive caregivers for others. (See 1 Corinthians 6:19-20)
    d. Delegate. Sometimes we must honor one another by asking others to share the load; being the expert on everything can be draining. (See Exodus 18:17-18.)

Jesus Christ is the Good Shepherd. He knows our names. He feels our pain. This Almighty Son of God took time to touch and heal lepers, to restore sight to blind beggars, and to raise a widow's son from the dead. Christ knows the draining effect of ministering to those who hurt. He left His work in our hands to pass on to this generation. Think of how much He loves us and wants to restore our joy and replenish our strength! We are whole people who are impacted in many ways by overwhelming situations. In order to stay healthy and avoid compassion fatigue, we must take responsibility for keeping our minds and bodies cared for and well.

Awareness and Skill Building

What comes to mind when you hear the word "awareness"? It is probably something along the lines of thinking, consciousness, or thoughtfulness—where someone is actively, mentally involved.

And what do you think about when you hear the term "skill set"? Perhaps you think about someone completing a task that requires certain skills—such as building a house, repairing a car, or creating a website. It involves the competency to complete complicated tasks.

With *Coaching in Context*, you will need to operate in awareness of the person being coached as well as follow the process, steps, and tasks that coaching demands. What you do requires *awareness*—building relationships. But it is also about *skill building*, using what you know to extend someone a helping hand. A positive coach can help stir up the gifts that are within men and women and help them set goals for their own futures.

At the same time, a coach must be alert to the continual need for their own growth and development and not allow their personal skills to atrophy. "If you're going to cut down a forest, it is better that you periodically stop and sharpen the saw before going back to work. The interruption for saw-sharpening may seem a nuisance. But without it, the saw will grow increasingly dull and will have decreased effectiveness" (Ron Jensen, *Make a Life, Not Just a Living*).

As a coach, you should keep your skills sharp and expect to see rewards in multiple dimensions in your own life.

Most of us think of coaching as the process of skill building—improving professionally in some aspect of vocation. But coaching has a much broader, wider, and all-encompassing purpose. Coaching is built to provide a variety of benefits. To increase efficiency and effectiveness, a positive coach will also want to consider *expanding awareness* of the benefits of having a constellation of coaches. An illustration would be if you have a medical problem, you would probably go to a specialist who has knowledge in your area of need. If you would like to write better, then you would ask a writing coach. If you want to develop your spiritual life, then you would find a person who models a godly lifestyle. If you have an emotional issue, then you would look for a person who has a gift in counseling—someone who has worked through some of their own emotional issues and can pour that wisdom into others.

By enlarging options, we are better able to move into uncharted territory and make important connections that can benefit the interests of other individuals in our expanding world. Wayne Gretzky, the noted hockey player, once said, "You miss 100 percent of the shots you don't take." Gretzky's advice is as relevant to coaching as it is to the hockey rink. In other words, recognizing and acting on your ability to grow in various areas will allow you to achieve greater results than you could otherwise enjoy. When you learn and grow, you have more to offer those you coach. Let coaching expand your awareness. Give room for your experiences and encounters to shape and change you, too.

CHAPTER 3

Knowing Others

We've talked about knowing God, and the significance of a relationship with Him, and hopefully now you know more about who you are. But how well do you know others? As believers, we are commanded to love one another. The apostle John wrote in 1 John 4:20 that we are to love one another, and indeed, asserts that if we do not love our brothers and sisters, we cannot possibly love God.

Every Christian has the potential for, and is commanded to be involved in, the process of encouraging and building up one another (1 Thessalonians 5:11; Hebrews 10:24-25). In intentional relationships like coaching, mentoring, and discipleship, we walk alongside those we train in order to encourage, equip, and challenge one another in love to grow toward maturity in Christ. This includes equipping those we train *to train others* as well. Discipleship means being a good steward of the *influence* God has given you for the purpose of improving the condition of others. Personal experiences and knowledge are great gifts to share.

Organized efforts by the Church can be used to assist personal growth as well. Coaches can help meet the ever-increasing demands in local churches to serve people. Such a ministry should be considered an essential part of the priesthood of all believers (1 Peter 2:5, 9).

Coaching, in particular, prepares someone to experience deeper levels of growth and maturity in an accelerated manner. Individuals thrive when they get the chance to develop their spiritual gifts. Every believer receives at least one spiritual gift (1 Corinthians 12:4-7, 11). God cheers us on when we develop and use what we have been given, right where we are. Great exploits usually have small beginnings. Faithfulness and diligence make the difference.

Serving Your Trainee

Coaches are leaders, and effective coaches lead best out of service and sacrifice. Again, the apostle John gives us an example: "*We ought to lay down our lives for our brothers and sisters*" (1 John 3:16). As coaches, we are to be motivated by love. It is love that will guide the effectiveness of our coaching and how well we get to know our clients. As leaders and coaches, we demonstrate our love with humility and vulnerability.

But what does this mean? In the New Testament, we see the term *diakonia* (servant, service) referring to people in leadership. (See Appendix D.)

Often, coaches are considered spiritually, emotionally, and psychologically "all-wise." Sometimes trainees will think of their issues as "fixable" simply because of their assumptions about the wisdom and experience of the coach. Coaches are rarely viewed as mere instruments and servants God uses to help shape people's lives. Instead, it might be tempting for trainees to put coaches on a pedestal, thinking they never struggle or need grace. But in reality, every coach is a forgiven sinner, just like the mentee. Our frailty and vulnerability are things we need to be open about with those we coach.

Build Leaders, Build Character

It is important to realize that coaching in context involves building leaders by building character. John C. Maxwell, in his book *The 21 Irrefutable Laws of Leadership*, regarding the law of influence, tells us that leadership requires character. "True leadership always begins with the inner person."

Those who approach you for coaching often are looking for improvement or insights on how to match their strengths to opportunities for growth in various areas of their life: intrapersonal (their own behavior or feelings), interpersonal relationships (relationships with others), or professional life (performance). Scripture speaks clearly to human struggles, illuminating both our inner battles and our outer troubles. Jesus Christ understands what is hard and perplexing about our lives. He meets us with grace and patiently sets about making us over. His example is a lesson to us. Remember: Successful coaching is about *character* and not *coercion* (Mark 10:42-45; Luke 22:25-27; 1 Peter 5:1-4), *submission*, not *hierarchy* (Hebrews 13:7).

-For Contemplation-

How is your character?
What action steps are you personally working
on to develop your character?
And how will you then foster strong character in your mentee?

What Is Your *Why?*

In 2009, Simon Sinek started a movement to help people become more inspired at work, and, in turn, to inspire their colleagues. Sinek uses an example he describes as the "Golden Circle" in his book *Start with Why.* According to Sinek, every organization knows "what" they do (to fulfill the organization's core beliefs), but the most essential element is knowing "why" they do what they do. For example, "Why does the organization exist?" We talk about "what" we do (results), we sometimes talk about "how" we do it (the process), but rarely do we articulate "why" we do what we do.

My good friend, Greg Campbell, put it this way in *The 5-2-1 Principle*:

> When we ask why, we approach a challenging issue with an open mind, determined to genuinely understand the reasons behind our direction, processes, or actions. Only by being willing to accept the results of going deep can we ascertain if we do, in fact, fully understand why we've been doing what we've been doing. Only then can we grasp how our current situation affects our ability to move forward.

When you coach, you will want to start with "why," because everyone was born with a purpose. You are most likely following the desires of your own heart and living out what you feel called to do. In coaching, especially as believers in Jesus, it is very important to know that a significant role for you is to assist the person you are coaching in finding or identifying their own assignment—their "why." Only then, with that sense of purpose, can they truly have the energy to keep going, to get up every morning to do what they've been assigned to do. Once you understand your purpose, you know your *why:* why you do what you do. The success of the person you are coaching will depend on their finding their "*why.*"

Being entrusted as a coach is a position not to be taken lightly. Equally important, the effective coach will not make broad assumptions about the trainee. As you gain experience and skills and begin to see the fruit of your effectiveness as a coach, there may be a tendency to develop a "plan" to impose on every person being coached who is facing similar challenges. Clients are not cookies; cookie cutter answers will not work. The wise coach will, instead, coach in context: spend time discerning the trainee's personal experiences and spiritual gifts. Then the coach will guide the person being coached in creating appropriate personalized approaches to the goal-setting process.

An old parable from India recounts the story of a group of blind men who encountered an elephant for the first time. Not knowing what an elephant looked like, they each gave an interpretation based on the part of the elephant they first encountered. "An elephant is like a spear," decided the man who felt the tusk. "I think the elephant is like a snake," said the man who had been probed by the trunk. One man happened to touch the tail. "I would say that an elephant is like a rope." Another grabbed the elephant around a knee. "I say the elephant resembles a tree," he concluded.

We smile at the limited perspective of the blind men. None is wrong, yet none is completely right either. Gifting perspectives are very similar. None of us has the entire perspective; we all have just a part. Getting a handle on a holistic perspective of the person you are coaching will be invaluable as you unpack their life experiences.

Be a "There you are" not a "Here I am" person. Always greet the person you are coaching with enthusiasm and warmth, encouraging them to feel at ease and at home during your meeting. Keep in mind that your attention and expertise belong to the one you are coaching. Be on time, prepared, and praying for the wisdom and coaching you need to transfer or share during this time.

How Do We Get There? Strategy and Action

Helping people set goals, plan action steps, and take steps to move forward with accountability involves leadership. Leadership does not wait to do something that should be done now. The longer you wait, you increase the odds that you will never actually do it. Coaching is as much about change as it is about leadership. And coaching is a valuable service that can illuminate and mobilize Christian leaders. Moreover, change and its implications for leadership are at the core of coaching. Coaching in context builds around a process involving three core tasks:

Assessment
Challenge
Support

These core elements may be in play at any time or in any order:

Assessment:

Assessment helps determine where the client is now. And understanding spiritual gifts is an aspect of coaching that is uniquely Christian. The Bible does not say much about strengths, but spiritual gifts are mentioned in several places. And when we truly surrender ourselves to the Personality of Jesus Christ, we discover a real personality of our own. C.S. Lewis in *Mere Christianity* made this point abundantly clear when he spoke to the far-reaching implications of our uniqueness in Christ:

> The more we get what we now call 'ourselves' out of the way and let Him take us over, the more truly ourselves we become. There is so much of Him that millions and millions of 'little Christs,' all different, will still be too few to express Him fully. He made them all. He invented—as an author invents characters in a novel—all the different men that you and I were intended to be.

Nonetheless, in a world that we may well try to "be myself," he goes on to say, "The more I resist Him and try to live on my own, the more I become dominated by my own heredity and upbringing and surroundings and natural desires. In fact, what I so proudly call 'Myself' becomes merely the meeting place for trains of events which I never started and which I cannot stop."

Stated another way, insights from a personality test are *poor substitutes* to our surrender to the Personality of Christ. Personality tests and assessments are simply *good supplements* for gaining insights into understanding our personality. Remember, God gave us each unique talents, gifts, and personalities that He can use to shape us into Jesus-like leaders. He could have made us all the same, but He didn't. So, no matter who you are or where you are starting from, we are all called to grow closer to Jesus and to deepen our relationships with one another.

So, how do we discover our own strengths or find strengths in the people we coach?

The apostle Paul, in 1 Corinthians, stressed the fact that it is by God's will that there are a variety of gifts given to individuals. Moreover, the Bible provides us with three lists of spiritual gifts in Ephesians 4, 1 Corinthians 12, and Romans 12. The purpose of the Holy Spirit's bestowing gifts upon believers is for the strengthening of these individuals for the practical work of ministry—to build up the body of Christ.

One of my mentors, Dr. Harold Sala, put it this way in *Getting Acquainted with the Holy Spirit:*

> When I think about spiritual gifts, I remember the manner in which I gave gifts to my three children as they were growing to maturity. Because I loved them equally, I tried to keep my gifts to them within the reach of equal value, but rarely if ever were my gifts to them identical. Why? Their ages, abilities, personalities, and interest were entirely different. The

gifts of a parent to his children are based on the need, personality, and the desires of the child.

The gifts described in Ephesians 4 are commonly called "Equipping Gifts," "Ministry Gifts," "5-Fold Gifts," or "Position Gifts." This list includes apostle, prophet, evangelist, pastor, and teacher—gifts of position for the ones who disciple and equip the Church as the Body of Christ.

In 1 Corinthians 12, we learn about the "Manifestation Gifts" or "Power Gifts." Sometimes they are referred to as "Charismatic Gifts." These gifts basically require that you be available as a vessel for the Holy Spirit to use.

The gifts listed in Romans 12 are called "Motivational Gifts" or "Personality Gifts," and they help explain why we do what we do. They are the permanent possession of every believer that shows how God wired us, and evidences are often apparent even in childhood.

While all these gifts are important, we focus on motivational gifts in the coaching process because they give us these powerful clues in key areas of life and leadership:

a. Enhancing communication: Knowing the different ways those with certain gifts approach communication can create powerful levels of understanding.
b. Resolving conflict: What happens when I understand the gifting of the other person and can look at the problem from their perspective.
c. Understanding roles that fit and do not fit: Appropriate jobs, volunteer roles, avoiding burnout.
d. Building teams: Understanding what gifts can best accomplish the task, and empowering others through using approaches that will probably work best within their unique giftedness.

A comprehensive understanding of spiritual gifts can be found in D.A. Carson's book, *Showing the Spirit: A Theological Exposition of 1 Corinthians 12-14.* An excellent treatment on discovering the presence and power of the Holy Spirit can be found in Harold J. Sala's book, *Getting Acquainted with the Holy Spirit.* For a practical treatment of motivational gifts, you will want an assessment tool. Several are available online. Books such as *Discover Your God-Given Gifts* by Don and Katie Fortune are also useful resources. Here's a brief recap of the motivational gifts:

These seven motivational gifts—prophecy, serving, teaching, encouraging (exhortation), giving, administration/leadership, and mercy—closely parallel personality types and serve as indicators of how a person being coached will successfully negotiate challenges and goals.

Prophecy: Those with this gift tend to see things in black and white and are concerned about what is *right*. They have the ability to hear clearly from God and communicate that to others.

Key characteristics: forthright, intuitive, righteousness, courage, introspective.

Areas for growth: tolerance, patience, optimism, humility.

Server: These are the people you want to have around because they want to serve others and are high-energy doers.

Key characteristics: helpful, meticulous, practical, present-oriented (can focus only on now), doers.

Areas for growth: tolerance, fidelity to family commitments, humility.

Teacher: Teacher-gifted individuals are emotionally stable people who love research and problem solving. Teachers of young children do not usually work from this gift—the teacher gift is more suited to college teaching and intellectually challenging pursuits.

Key characteristics: inquisitive, analytical, systematic, even-tempered, objective, principled.

Areas for growth: prudence, openness to new viewpoints, acceptance, flexibility, focus.

Encourager: Encouragers (exhorters) are highly relational and adept communicators who love to encourage and challenge others to reach their full potential.

Key characteristics: verbal, encouraging, pragmatic, relational, creative, optimistic.

Areas for growth: truthfulness, humility, empathy, supportive.

Givers: Givers are naturally generous people with a knack for making money and making the most of what they have.

Key characteristics: industrious, strive for excellence, financial expertise, generous, hospitable.

Areas for growth: generosity, balance, dependability, prudence, graciousness.

Leader/administrator: Natural leaders who enjoy organizing people and projects. They are people of vision and inspire others to get involved.

Key characteristics: goal-oriented, visionary, delegate well, organized, determined.

Areas for growth: empathy, unhurriedness, vulnerability, consistency, integrity, promise keeping.

Mercy: Those with this gift bring love, thoughtfulness, and sensitivity into relationships. They believe the best in people and are attracted to hurting people.

Key characteristics: caring, sensitive, self-sacrificing, empathetic, feeling-oriented.

Areas for growth: boldness, courage, forgiveness, merciful.

Understanding these basic personal dynamics gives us keen insights into our own lives as well as those we coach. Here are several scenarios to give us examples of this principle:

1. Imagine a teacher-gifted husband, who is practical and emotionally distant, married to a mercy-gifted woman who wonders about his affections for her because he thinks things she's looking for, like flowers and romantic getaways, are impractical and unnecessary. Great strides can be made when he understands her needs, and she knows that she needs to appreciate even small steps he takes in her direction.

2. You need to build a team. Rather than choose your best friend, the server who's always willing, or the person you think owes you one, make your decisions from the perspective of what gifts you will need to accomplish your tasks.

3. Someone comes to you for coaching because he or she has just lost a job. Clients who are outspoken (such as those with gifts like a teacher, encourager, and prophet) will automatically start searching for work, scouring the Internet, etc. They will mainly need help defining what they are looking for and what goals to set. Others with gifts like mercy and service

will need help getting through the rejection of losing the job and wallowing in that perceived rejection.

4. A question to reflect on when helping a person being coached to set goals: What goals are appropriate for the person?

There are several tools to help you see your unique design through a biblical lens: DISC Profile, Myers-Briggs Temperament Inventory, the online assessment at: quoir.com/Walt-Russell.html, and others are all helpful. These tools can give you insights into yourself and help in building loving relationships with others that Jesus envisioned.

Use the information from these tests to your best advantage. And, although several strength-finding inventories exist, we should not overlook a great resource—simply asking people to list their strengths, including asking them to get feedback from people who know them best. One of the most important things to remember is to encourage those you coach in their gifts and strengths, but always in context of humble appreciation toward the Giver of our gifts.

Challenge:

Coaches empower people to set and reach goals. Good coaching is concentrated on bringing about greater awareness and then stimulating intentionality toward positive action. And because public awareness and peer pressure are great motivators, it can be helpful if the people who want change state publicly what they plan to do and indicate who will hold them accountable. It helps, as well, to remember that it is often easier to make a slight change than it is to make a big, dramatic change. Often bigger changes may have unintended consequences that can create drastic disruptions in areas that did not need to be changed in the first place.

Coaches help people to accept change. At other times, they gently encourage people to make changes. But people are not usually motivated to change until the benefits of going through it are greater than the benefits of things staying the way they are. When this happens, the coach provides feedback, a unique perspective, and when appropriate, a nudge toward moving in the direction of accomplishing their goals. At these pivotal moments of transition, we seek to apply what we believe to ourselves, and to really allow Christ to impact our minds, our lives, our emotions, and our imaginations. We must always trust in the power of the Holy Spirit and focus on what He can do through us rather than focusing on our limitations.

Moreover, coaching develops people in the church to help meet the pastoral care needs within a church—an essential part of the priesthood of all believers (1 Peter 2:5, 9). The ripple effect we'll see from coaching won't appear overnight, but it will happen. As the old saying goes, "Plans are only good intentions unless they immediately degenerate into hard work." – Peter Drucker

Support:

Everyone has God-given talents that He desires us to use to good effect wherever we are. Individuals thrive and flourish when they are challenged with opportunities to grow their talents and to receive support and encouragement as their God-given talents are shaped and refined. In this sense, coaching can lead people into the exploration of both their inner lives and their outer worlds, making sure head and heart and hands go together.

Some people want a coach who will tell them what to do and where to go and focus on solving problems. Instead, coaching in context concentrates on building people up by supporting them. Encouraging clients to envision what could be by using focused questions to stimulate their thinking will let them discover God's leading themselves. Focusing on building relationships (being a positive and supportive role model) can greatly increase the potential for providing sustained hope and inspiration toward positive change.

The Word of God and experience have taught us that it is much easier to carry a burden when there are men and women who come alongside us and help carry part of the load. But support is not about fixing or pressuring people to do something they really do not want to do. The purpose of support is to provide a context in which people can grow and change. Support can benefit everyone by helping people avoid the pitfalls others have already experienced. Coaching offers encouragement and support to those who have accepted the challenges and opportunities of integrating their faith into all areas of their life.

Building Relationships with Affirmation and Transparency

Coaches have a unique relationship with those they coach, and once they have established trust, they are in a position to influence and affect the trainee. Thoughtless criticism can damage the trainee's self-perspective. That's why it is imperative that as a coach you consistently affirm them. Build a strong relationship with them by developing positive interactions, walking with them during challenging times, prayerfully listening, mutually confessing, and affirming their gifts and talents.

Transparency is vital for effective coaching, because the extent to which we are willing to reveal to others the areas of our lives that need God's transforming touch is the extent to which we are inviting the Holy Spirit to make us new. Our personal truth is the foundation upon which core values are built and where purpose and performance link together. When coaching someone, it's important to remember that we grow most when we are helping others grow; we must be willing to share our own reasons to change. And our relationship with the Holy Spirit, focused on transformation through repentance, relationship, and accountability, will provide a model for those we coach so they can coach others, too.

Now is the time to remember and apply what you learned from the personal assessment you completed in the previous section.

Experienced coaches recognize that the areas where they have experienced the most failure often become their strongest areas of character and ministry. It is important to "tell the whole story," the failures and victories, in order to effectively testify about God's redeeming power at work through difficult experiences.

Sharing your personal stories in coaching sessions is intended to act as a catalyst for your trainee to share theirs, so brevity is the rule. Identify crucial moments in your life and learn to communicate them succinctly. Focus on the principle you gleaned that led to your personal victory, not the details.

Dignity and Depravity

As growth and transformation begin to take place in our lives and in the lives of our trainees, we must not lose sight (or allow our trainees to lose sight) of the terrible and wonderful reality of the human condition: our depravity and dignity.

In the Old Testament, Adam and Eve were given the commandment to not eat from the "tree of the knowledge of good and evil" (Genesis 2:16-17). In answering a question regarding the "Greatest Commandment," Jesus combined two commandments. The first was to love God, and the second was to love others as we love ourselves. Still, we often find ourselves running from God (violating the Greatest Commandment), which often results in broken relationships and unresolved conflict with others (violating the Second Greatest Commandment). As American writer, theologian, and Trappist monk, Thomas Merton once pointed out, "Man is not at peace with his fellow man because he is not at peace with himself, and he is not at peace with himself because he is not at peace with God."

God created human beings with needs for intimacy, needs that He designed to be met in relationship with Himself and other human beings. Intimacy with God is found as we abide in Christ and is the prerequisite for true intimacy with others. Satan, on the other hand, seeks to entice us to meet our need for intimacy through destructive, selfish, and illegitimate ways.

The human condition is a story of both the best and worst of people. The Gospel holds both of these realities in tension, and we should strive to do the same in our coaching. Being both *image-bearers* (Genesis 1:26-27) and *broken people* (Romans 3:23) can help explain our troubling duality. When we overemphasize our sinfulness, it becomes easy to miss the God-given dignity bestowed on every man and woman as His image-bearers. But we should also be cautious of over-emphasizing human depravity, because both *dignity* and *depravity* are part of the human condition. We cannot minimize either.

Abiding in the Vine

In the metaphor of the vine and the branches found in John 15, Jesus Christ is the True Vine and believers are the branches of this Vine. The great truth in this chapter speaks of the living union between Christ and those who believe and abide in Him. That union with Christ supports our spiritual life and results in our life producing fruit. He compares His Father to the gardener to let us know that His people are not only under His care, but under His Father's care as well.

In horticulture, roots serve a variety of functions, including nourishing the plant by absorbing moisture and minerals as well as providing support for the plant. The metaphor of the vine includes the roots, and just as the root is unseen, our lives as believers and branches of the True Vine are hidden in Christ. It is in and through Him that all nourishment and support are supplied to us. As such, Truth (of which the natural vine is a figure) is fulfilled in Jesus. We will be unable to bear fruit without the constant support and nourishment of the True Vine.

When the branches are abiding in the vine, they are all rooted in the One Vine and in this natural community; we are never alone but are interconnected with each other and with Him. Life flows from the root, through the stem, to the farthest leaves on the outstretched branches, who are all bearing fruit for His Kingdom.

The metaphor of the vine and branches also applies to coaching. Because we live in an imperfect world, problems and challenges threaten the health of our Christian growth and unity, just as pests, disease, and inclement weather threaten the health of the vineyard, as every gardener knows.

Similar difficulties will arise in coaching sessions. But always remember, coaching is accomplished in context, which involves considering a range of variables that can impact your relationship with your trainee. Just a few examples include the location, time of day, relationships, behavior, feelings, and even things like trust, integrity, and respect.

Many church leaders are trained to study God's Word, but they are not trained to study His world. Coaches must not only be wise interpreters of God's Word but also wise interpreters of the culture of those they serve. An effective coach must be like the group of men in ancient Israel who knew what Israel should do because they understood their times. *"From Issachar, men who understood the times and knew what Israel should do"* (1 Chronicles 12:32 NIV).

CHAPTER 4

The Practice and
Power of Prayer

Prayer takes us to God's Throne Room, where the sovereign King of the Universe waits to meet with us personally. Prayer is not an escape from the harsh realities of life or an earned privilege from our own works or merit. Prayer is an intimate abiding in Jesus Christ and a fundamental act of relationship built on mutual love.

Some think of prayer as a celestial award ceremony where we get a trophy for showing up to meet with God. I know what that feels like. I have too often approached my Bible reading and prayer times as an achievement-oriented spiritual discipline carried out by my sheer will power. There are times that I have to remind myself that my prayer time is something I do "with God," not just "for God" in order to serve or satisfy my ego.

Looking back at such prideful and self-centered moments, I realize what a precious experience I missed—the chance to be in the presence of Abba (Daddy) and be refreshed by the comforting and healing my soul needs most. Every time I spend time in His presence, Christ enables me, through the power of the Holy Spirit, to find joy in loving God and the people around me in a way that brings glory to Him.

"The Spirit you received does not make you slaves, so that you live in fear again; rather, the Spirit you received brought about your adoption to sonship. And by him we cry, 'Abba, Father'" (Romans 8:15-16 NIV).

God has given you an all-important place in His redeeming work in this world. He created you for that place, equipped you to fulfill His unique plan for you, and desires that you give Him first place in whatever you plan to accomplish. Successful coaching doesn't come from reading an instruction manual—no matter how thorough it might be. Coaching is successful when you access the power found through abiding in the Living Word, who furnishes all you could ever need of God's love, grace, righteousness, power, and goodness.

These virtues set the stage for everything else God has in store for your life. God's kingdom work for you is supported through prayer. You can pray expectantly, because by God's grace, the Holy Spirit fills you and empowers you to do His work.

"For we are His workmanship, created in Christ Jesus for good works, which God prepared beforehand, that we should walk in them" (Ephesians 2:10).

Learning to Become More Prayerful

Prayer is part of the spiritual food that nourishes us each day and is a necessary part of the Christian life. We must be fed, but figuring out the amount and frequency is up to the individual and the Holy Spirit. Our prayer time can also help us get a better perspective on the goals we set, as well as our timelines for accomplishing them. An effective way to become a person of prayer is to set a time and a place to meet with God every day. Choose a time that fits best in your schedule. You may find the best time for prayer is early morning, as Jesus often did, before your day takes on a frenzied pace. (See Mark 1:35.) Making prayer a daily habit is also easier if you have a quiet place where you will not be interrupted. This is *your* time to talk with God!

To help focus your thoughts on what to talk to God about, or whom to pray for, keep a notebook and your Bible near the place you've chosen to pray. The next thing to do is choose those for whom you will pray. Write one name on each line, with specific requests for that person on the line beside the name. As coaches, I strongly urge you to pray for those you coach. There are times when you may not be able to pray out loud with the people you coach, but you can always pray for them silently.

In our ongoing friendship with Jesus Christ we bring our coaching efforts into our prayers and learn how to perceive what He is saying to us; that is the nature of friendship. We trust that God is interested in our coaching efforts and will be working with us on the transforming work we are doing and providing us with the direction that we need. Have a sense of expectancy. Look forward to talking things over with your Heavenly Father and hearing His response. You can also pray and ask for God's guidance *while* you are coaching. These prayers can be done silently during your session.

Learning how to hear God takes practice, and fortunately there are a number of valuable resources available to help enhance this aspect of our relationship with God. F.B. Meyer's *The Secret of Guidance*, John Eldridge's *Walking With God*, and Dallas Willard's *Hearing God* are just a few books that can inform and guide you in this important part of your coaching.

When prayer takes on a regular rhythm in your life, you'll be safeguarded from forgetting about God when you succeed or turning away from Him when you fail. Prayer will help you consistently abide in God instead of phasing in and out of God's love, based on your feelings or performance. Spending time in prayer can transform your entire life as God gives you His perspective. As C.S. Lewis wrote in *Mere Christianity*, "The more we get what we now call 'ourselves' out of the way and let Him take us over, the more truly ourselves we become."

Imagine what a difference talking things over with God every day will make in your life and your coaching. The reason is the Source of prayer's power. Prayer connects you with the Sovereign God of the Universe; you rest in His power, not your own. *"The prayer of a righteous man is powerful and effective"* (James 5:16).

A New Perspective

Try to avoid the belief that Jesus' job is to shield you from all struggles or adversity. The truth is, as James 1:2 says, *"Consider it all joy, my brethren, when you encounter various trials, knowing that the testing of your faith produces endurance, and let endurance have its perfect result, that you may be perfect and complete, lacking in nothing."* Trials are a part of life. Daily prayer will, with God's help, make you fit and strong enough to face whatever comes your way. *"Devote yourselves to prayer, keeping alert in it with an attitude of thanksgiving"* (Colossians 4:2).

Prayer in Coaching

Pray before you start a coaching session, while you are coaching, and after you have finished. Remember that prayer is simply a conversation with God that involves both talking to Him and listening to Him. You do not have to use lofty sounding words or a different tone of voice. Simply invite God to be present in the coaching experience. You can pray with confidence—even if you think you do not have the right words. The apostle Paul tells us, *"The Spirit helps us in our weakness,"* adding, *"We do not know what to pray for as we ought, but the Spirit himself intercedes for us with groanings too deep for words"* (Romans 8:26).

Prayer is also a powerful tool for discerning God's will. God invites His people to approach Him through prayer in every situation (Philippians 4:6). Moreover, God's Word assures us that He hears and answers our prayers (Psalm 17:6; Proverbs 15:29; 1 John 5:14-15). So, before you start a coaching session, surrender your coaching plans to God and ask them to be shaped and perfected by Him. When you accept responsibility for aiding another person's spiritual journey, be sure to get God's approval and guidance at every step. Trust God to guide your choices and decisions. Ask Him to show you the best steps forward and for the power of the Holy Spirit to fulfill them. Trust Him to supply your coaching needs and guide your coaching efforts.

Below is the kind of prayer you might offer to God before a coaching session:

> *Help me to lovingly serve the person I'm coaching as a person—not as a project. Help me to remove the obstacles, either in my attitude or actions that might keep me from learning or teaching the things You want me to learn or teach. Open my heart and the heart of _____ (insert name) to be sensitive to Your voice. Help me desire to do Your will, knowing that Your will always works out for my greater good and Your highest glory. Amen.*

Prayer is an opportunity for us to grow closer to God, as we rely upon Him to guide the choices and decisions we make in daily living. We pray not just to get something from Him—an easier life or a request that everything can go smoothly—but for a closer daily walk with Him.

For Reflection

Remember, self-reliance in our ability to be consistent in Bible study and prayer can easily turn into legalism. I like what Dallas Willard said at an international conference several years ago regarding Bible reading and spiritual disciplines. He talked about a process of "embedding connection points with Christ into our daily life." His point was that practicing the presence of Christ puts us in a continual attitude of receiving and drawing upon God's grace throughout the day and not limited to a scheduled event. This is an attitude toward prayer that spills out into our relationships with other people throughout the day.

> *"I keep asking that the God of our Lord Jesus Christ,
> the glorious Father, may give you the Spirit of wisdom
> and revelation, so that you may know him better. I pray
> that the eyes of your heart may be enlightened in order
> that you may know the hope to which he has called you,
> the riches of his glorious inheritance in his holy people,
> and his incomparably great power for us who believe."*
> (Ephesians 1:17-19 NIV)

CHAPTER 5

Communicating Effectively

Every day we talk. Every day we have conversations. Every day we communicate.

What is the first thing you think about when you hear the word "communication"? Most likely, you think about someone talking, or two people having a conversation. You may think about what is being communicated or how. However, talking is only half of a conversation. The other half is listening.

As a coach, over half of your communication with the person you are coaching should be listening. Many coaches believe their role in coaching is to instruct, to convey, or to teach the person being coached what they are supposed to do in order to transform their lives. However, the fundamental tool of coaching in context is asking questions. People are made for self-discovery. Indeed, the Socratic method of teaching is rooted in asking the student questions, allowing the student time for exploration and self-discovery.

Listening Attentively

The listening skills of a good coach, when complemented with asking effective questions, insightful observations, and affirming feedback, can lead to greater insights for the trainee. The coach's role is to hear what is being said intellectually, as well as what is communicated between the lines, often referred to as "subtext." Many people, and too often many coaches, when they are "listening" are waiting, with bated breath, to reply, based on what they want to say, teach, or tell. Good coaches seek first to understand and will set aside their personal agendas to be fully attentive to their client. Asking good questions is the first step in becoming an effective listener.

So, as a coach, you will need to listen well and ask effective questions. I recommend asking follow-up questions or asking for clarification whenever you need greater clarity. Think about these points as you work with others. Doing so will help you develop more productive listening habits:

1. Stay focused: Instead of thinking about how you will respond, listen carefully to what is said, try to consider what the other person actually means by what they are saying. Ask clarifying questions. (Tune in to hearing the Holy Spirit as well.)
2. Take your time: Honor what is being said by taking time to contemplate and consider their words. Affirm their contribution to the conversation and repeat back what you've heard.

Holy Spirit-led Conversations

Believers in Jesus accept God as three persons in one—the Trinity. We value the presence of the Holy Spirit in our lives. Indeed, Jesus called the Holy Spirit "the Comforter" and the importance of seeking His presence in a coaching session cannot be overstated.

Because every person is uniquely created, there is no one-size-fits-all coaching solution or model. Coaching is not a process or a formula to be applied the same way to each trainee. What works for one individual may not work for another, and assuming that the process will be similar for all will do a grave disservice to those we coach. Therefore, it is imperative that we rely on the Holy Spirit for guidance. Let's look at how we can learn to discern what the trainee's needs are in cooperation with the Holy Spirit.

"But everyone must be quick to hear, slow to speak, and slow to anger" (James 1:19). This Scripture is very appropriate for us. We must listen, listen, listen until we understand the context from which our trainee is speaking. We must also listen to the Holy Spirit and His direction for the conversation. Careful discernment of the coaching conversation will help us understand what approaches to take with the mentee.

The following acrostics, (LISTENER) and (SPEAKER), identify some important clues to listening well and responding appropriately:

Listen attentively.

Interrupting dishonors the trainee and is prohibited.

Speaker's experience is the point of focus, not yours.

Train yourself to be aware of your nonverbal responses.

Engage in the listening process until you have fully understood.

Never defend yourself, argue, explain, or problem-solve.

Enter the perspective/mindset of the speaker through empathy and compassion.

Respond with empathy and respect.

Let each one of you speak the truth with his neighbor, for we are members one of another (Ephesians 4:25 ESV).

State your feelings/explain your experiences.

Practice honesty/speak the truth in love (without minimizing or pretending).

Employ "I" statements rather than "you" statements.

Avoid anger by taking a "time-out" as a way to cool down, not to escape the conversation.

Keep destructive blame games, accusations, and name-calling out of the conversation.

Engage in the process with vulnerability, even if painful or difficult.

Realize the feelings underlying your anger, like hurt or sadness.

Ask, Don't Tell Strategy

Jesus asked 307 questions because asking engages others in conversation and thought. The saying "Ask, don't tell!" is a great reminder to a coach. It will probably take some time to learn to "ask" rather than "tell," but there are great rewards for doing so. Why is asking rather than telling so important?

- The person being coached knows far more about their life than the coach will ever know.
- Research suggests that people are more motivated to carry out their own ideas and solutions.
- Asking lets the person being coached know that their opinions are important and that you take them seriously. This can be empowering.
- Asking shows that you honor and value your trainee.

Questions that we ask as coaches set the tone for our interaction with the trainee. Avoid "yes" and "no" questions and begin by trusting the Holy Spirit to lead you to the right question for the situation at hand.

Good contextualization of questions requires good listening and careful observation. The key is learning to ask appropriate questions that are relevant to the situation. Appropriate questions tend to strongly affirm people, use language that conveys genuine concern and caring, and are spoken with the best interest of everyone in mind. If you are unsure or want to verify something that was said, you can use a "reflection" question and "reflect" to the person being coached what you heard. For example, "What I hear you saying is…" or "Can you expand?" or even, "Help me to understand."

Communicating Within a Wider Context

As the world around us shrinks and exposure to other worldviews becomes commonplace, you'll find yourself coaching people with different cultural norms and ways of speaking. It is easy to assume that other people think like you and speak like you, but misunderstandings in a coaching session are simply inevitable. This can be true even when you are coaching someone from a background very similar to your own. When misunderstandings occur, seek to understand and find common ground. Ask yourself, "What will help me better understand where this person is coming from?" (Their *context*).

Even the use of a simple word can be misunderstood. For example, if I was using the word "trunk" in a conversation about my car, I'd interpret the word much differently than if I was talking about a tree or the "nose" of an elephant. Just as the word "treat" in a medical conversation with a doctor means something different than if you were talking about goodies for your kids.

Coaching in context is about learning to seek common ground and building relationships with people. And when it comes to coaching, if a person doesn't feel understood, he or she will be reluctant to fully engage in the coaching process. We're all different, with unique designs, divergent functions, and different experiences (Romans 12:4-5). So, even though the *nuances* of cross-cultural contextualization are beyond the intended scope of this book, *Coaching in Context* seeks to bridge cultural gaps as an integral part of effective coaching.

CHAPTER 6

Coaching Tips for Implementing SMART Goals

Vision and Goal Setting

Vision not only involves discerning God's call for how we can serve other people in His Name but also becoming the kind of person God intends. When you coach, you are developing current and potential leaders, helping them to accomplish God's purpose for their life and the godly character they need to fulfill that vision. So beware of coaching that is focused too much on competence (doing) and too little on character (being). As Dallas Willard points out in *Renovation of The Heart*, vision involves a clear picture of the future ministry that God has placed on the heart of a leader: "If we are to be spiritually formed in Christ, we must have and must implement the appropriate vision, intention, and means. Not just any path we take will do...."

Vision involves the trainee asking, "What am I called to accomplish with my life?" And then, they need to desire a future of becoming more like Jesus Christ and being called and led by God to intentionally influence and bless those within their spheres of influence. Their vision informs the goals they set and the path of transformation they must follow to be fully equipped to fulfill that vision. God's vision for His people is always so much bigger than ours.

Helping a person envision who they are to become, where they want to go, or what they want to do is critical when coaching. I particularly like George Barna's definition of vision: "You might define vision as foresight with insight based on hindsight."

A vision should be a vivid, clear, and compelling guide that includes an easily communicated plan with enough detail to help the trainee to stay focused and motivated. For example, let's say that your trainee's vision is to "Proclaim the Gospel of Jesus Christ." While such a vision is noble, clear, understandable, and concise, it is too general to act upon. What this attained goal will actually look like is hard to say.

What is needed is more specifics and clarity about the end state they picture. The first critical step in helping the person you are coaching to create a vision or picture of their "end state" or "end goal" is to ensure the vision has enough detail to move on to the next step: to establish the goals and objectives that will actually get them where they want to go and become the person they envision.

The Importance of Character

Achieving goals allow your trainee to build a little of their future vision into their present-day work. Little by little their goals will help them fulfill their vision. *Coaching in Context* is designed to help them discover how to build their own leadership and coaching skills and equip them with tools that encourage insight and growth.

One of the most important intangibles regarding goal setting is the kind of person they are becoming—their internal character development. That is why *Coaching in Context* emphasizes character development as integral to coaching. It is not just about activity centered on tangible accomplishments. Remember, the goals they accomplish are not nearly as important as the person they are becoming by developing their character.

After writing down their vision (goals and character traits), they will need to create an action plan for bringing their vision into reality. Helping people set goals, plan action steps, and take the needed steps to move forward with the accountability needed involves leadership. Accountability is where vision meets action and accountability needs a plan—a tracking system that will help promote accountability. The plan can be as simple as an Excel spreadsheet of action items and tasks or as complex as a software tool that tracks tasks and goal status.

Goal setting helps us envision and plan for the future by translating vision into reality. Goal setting involves implementing the vision by asking, "What I am going *to do* to get there?" Asking the trainee, "What is going to make your goals, your "end state," a reality, and what will it take to make that happen?" will help to generate tasks and goals that will create the mechanism through which they can be held accountable for the goals they set.

"Plans are only good intentions unless they immediately degenerate into hard work." – Peter Drucker

SMART Goals (an acronym for Specific, Measurable, Attainable, Relevant, Time-bound) are structured to help work out the details of a plan and keep track of progress as the goals and vision are accomplished. When someone writes out specific SMART goals, they set a clear path for accomplishing them. Failing to put the vision and goals in writing will most likely cause them to remain *theoretical good intentions*.

The coach being guided by the Holy Spirit and God's truth as they help the trainee develop their SMART Goals will activate a sense of intentionality within your client. This will help them recognize the importance of SMART Goals for achieving their vision.

Setting goals and achieving them are important aspects of helping people grapple with the question, "What do I want to achieve?" But before moving forward in this section on SMART Goals, some important questions to ask your trainee would be, "Are you giving much thought to the things that really count?" "What kind of person do you want to become?" and "Do you expect God to arrange circumstances so that the very target you and He have decided on will begin to take shape internally and externally?"

What do SMART Goals look like? And how do you help those you coach to achieve them?

In George T. Doran's article, "There's a S.M.A.R.T. Way to Write Management's Goals and Objectives," he introduces the concept of SMART Goals. Doran explains that following the acronym is a simple way, a *smart* way, to write down one's objectives (vision or mission) and make them meaningful and actionable. In other words, it shows practical and possible ways to carry them out. Doran's system was in the context of business management, but we can leverage this tool to help those we coach be SMART with their own spiritual and emotional goals in the areas they're seeking growth and improvement.

The concept of SMART Goals is especially useful when it is combined with vision. Together these tools create a *holistic* approach to goal setting. The final product is not simply individual, disconnected pieces, but rather one coherent and unified picture of a vision fulfilled. Remember to keep your focus on the individual you're coaching, not just on the goals being set. Helping individuals succeed by accomplishing their goals *and* helping them to grow spiritually are inextricably linked as God's grace helps to accomplish both.

The following examples of **SMART: Specific, Measurable, Attainable, Relevant, and Time-bound Goals** are included to give you a more complete sense of how to help those you coach fill out the worksheet in Appendix B.

Identifying Personal Goals

SPECIFIC: Be specific. An individual should have a clear goal in mind, or at least specify an area for improvement. What do they seek to accomplish? Remember, the specific actions they outline should tie back in to their "end goal" or vision.

As a coach, this is the space to allow individuals to explore big dreams. Here you can give insight into the present to help them shape their future. And this is the time to help individuals not only explore, but also *sharpen* their vision. Encourage them to seek God's perspective and purpose for their life. This is best accomplished by urging them to develop a consistent lifestyle of prayer. (See Proverbs 14:26.) At this point, they need to focus on their priorities, remembering what the Bible says in Luke 12:34: *"For where your treasure is, there will your heart be also."*

You help individuals become visionary thinkers by challenging them to do things better and to make an impact. Being specific involves providing direction by helping others bring clarity to their plans, both in conceiving and in believing. For the trainees you coach to be engaged, they need to see how you are helping them to realize their goals.

Remember, what God has in store for His people is greater than anything we can dream of. Being specific is about catching a vision of what God has for us. And we can know if we are on the right track if we seek to do things that build people up (1 Thessalonians 5:11) If as a coach your goal is simply to help individuals climb higher than others on the ladder of success, you are doing them a disservice.

None of us can achieve our goals or accomplish anything of importance without clarity and intentionality. Vague wishes get us nowhere, so make sure your trainees craft concrete goals to accomplish. A crucial step in helping them get energized by their vision is to ask: "Is your goal specific, and will achieving this goal get you closer to achieving your vision?" This simple question can be a game changer.

MEASURABLE: To gain clarity, individuals should ask themselves: "Is my goal measurable? If not, how can I measure my progress along the way?"

It is one thing to set a goal, and another to make that goal clear and measurable. This step is where you encourage individuals to convert their goals into action steps, translating them into doable, bite-sized pieces. Here they implement a plan to take *small measurable steps* that will carry them closer to accomplishing their mission. This is also where you help them weed out unnecessary activities that detract or sidetrack their efforts. They might *want* to read their Bible more, for instance, but *what*, *when*, and *how* will they actually make that happen?

You might encourage those you coach to block off time on their calendar to focus on one single important task at a time.

ATTAINABLE: In order to help individuals improve the *probability* of seeing positive results, ask them: "Is your goal actually attainable? Who are the key people who will make it happen?"

We should never be afraid to dream big dreams, knowing that if God is asking us to do something, it *is* attainable. Remind those you coach that our assurance rests in knowing that the promise Jesus gave the disciples when He sent them out into the world is also ours: *"I am with you always"* (Matthew 28:20). We cannot allow fear to hold us back. If we never try, we will never succeed.

This is also the moment when the coach asks the hard questions. Ask them how many times they've looked back at goals they have set and asked, "Why in the world did I set this goal? What was I thinking?" The reality of goal setting is that there will be times when the goals individuals choose will be perceived as unattainable. Sometimes it is because the goals are simply unrealistic. But most often it is because they lose sight of their vision due to delays and/ or discouraging forces. Moreover, when individuals are not able to measure up to the goals they set for themselves, it is easy to quit in discouragement. A goal being attainable involves more than just the *probability* of accomplishing the goal. It requires them asking, "Can I reasonably do this?" Encourage those you coach to be humble enough to get some input, to do research, and to be willing to learn from others.

Attainable is used as a realistic evaluation of what it will take to accomplish goals. This is not about being afraid to fail, because failing is common, no matter how hard a person tries to avoid it. Reality says that they cannot accomplish what they want to all the time, so the coach needs to help them discern expectation from reality. Reality will help them make the necessary adjustments to accomplish the goals they need to make to reach their vision. It is not possible to be able to do or know everything. We can help our trainee develop new strengths by identifying and addressing their weaknesses.

If their goal, for example, is to build a skyscraper, or to design a rocket that will reach Mars, they will inevitably have to be open to focus on what they *do not* know rather than what they *do* know. It is okay to not know something and not worry about being able to accomplish everything they want to do. It is okay to simply look at their goals objectively and be willing to make changes when necessary. We can use the coaching process to add fresh perspective based on the experiences of others. It requires more wisdom to make necessary adjustments and changes than it does to try to force reality to change.

The person you are coaching will rise to the level of your expectations. Yet, some goals may not be attainable because the person you are coaching is not sufficiently motivated to do what it takes to reach the goal. Other times, it may be that they just do not have the capacity, skill, or ability to do what it takes. Your insights may help them discern which it is. Trying harder and overextending can lead to stress, burnout, and even depression. Sometimes saying "no" to a new opportunity can be the healthiest choice because it honors existing commitments and improves the likelihood of accomplishing current and future goals.

Edward Everett Hale once wrote, "I am only one, but I am one. I cannot do everything, but I can do something. And I will not let what I cannot do interfere with what I can do." Remember, persistence involves getting back up every time you fall. *"For though the righteous fall seven times, they rise again"* (Proverbs 24:16). Do not let discouragement rob your trainee of their destiny. With God's power, they can accomplish things they never would have accomplished in their own strength.

RELEVANT: For individuals to be more effective and efficient in staying on target, they need to ask: "Are these activities or tasks related to accomplishing my end state or vision?" and "How do I get from here to there without getting bogged down by the chaos of everyday life?"

The point of this exercise is not just that trainees reach their immediate goals; it is also about their intentionality and aligning their goals to their *overall vision.* Setting goals that track with the trajectory of their vision involves the practice of intentionality. It answers the question, "What can I do to align my actions with my values?" Sometimes, before setting new goals, it will be necessary for those you coach to reevaluate activities that have not been fruitful and make room for new things that can be fruitful.

As a coach you become the "how to" influencer of your trainees by helping them put "feet" to their vision and helping them mobilize their action plans. Remind them they do not have to say "yes" to everything—especially if it doesn't relate to their vision. Their goals are constrained by certain limits. What they do must be related to what will help them achieve their specific vision. Guide them into determining efforts they can make to focus on their goals and keep them from becoming distracted. Accomplishing anything takes determination. *"We must pay the most careful attention, therefore, to what we have heard, so that we do not drift away"* (Hebrews 2:1).

Endeavor to help those you coach make sure their goals are consistent with God's Word and their values. Once they take the time to evaluate their goals by determining how they support their vision, they will find that they have to say "no" to other opportunities. Here the important questions to ask them are: "Does this goal advance your vision?" If the answer is "'yes,'" ask, "Is there something else you're currently doing that you will have to give up by adding this to your schedule?" If the answer is "no," they must ask themselves why they're still doing it. (See Proverbs 20:25.) They must remember that they cannot do everything. They must continually evaluate their goals to ensure they are in alignment with their vision.

TIME-BOUND: If trainees want to be more intentional about accomplishing their goals, ask them: "Is your goal time-bound? When will results be achieved?"

Few components are as necessary for a job well done as adequate preparation, and that includes setting time limits for accomplishing small steps along the way. Good intentions typically benefit no one. When it comes to this stage in the sequence of setting SMART Goals, "Time frames" act as a roadmap with milestones, plotted for the completion of small steps. Goals are not accomplished with one giant leap, so helping those you coach to establish a time frame for action, moving their goals from paper to actionable steps, is an important element for success. Make it clear that they cannot just write and talk about what they want to do; they must act.

Reaching goals that are in alignment with their mission will require a multipronged, sustained effort that is actualized by incremental movements in the right direction. Time framing involves looking at the long-term timetable for completion. Like the pull of gravity, there will naturally be a myriad of things that will compete for the valuable commodities of their time and attention. So encourage the person you are coaching to stay focused on their top priorities, making a list of them in order of importance.

The key is not to lose sight of the goals as they take steps to reach them, being patient with the process, and yet consistently focused on each goal. The day-to-day markers are where the grace of God will be experienced in your client's daily walk. One aspect of Time-bound can be easily missed when you do not help those you coach to think in terms of experiencing the *process* and not just the *product* of goal setting, i.e., seeing goal setting as a means of managing *life* and not just managing *time*.

Granted, focus and clarity accelerate the potential for your trainees reaching their goals. Just as vagueness and confusion accelerate the potential for not having goals become a reality. By using SMART Goals, your trainees will learn about using time frames to accomplish goals. Remember, however, that character development is a lifelong process.

Faith is important, but biblical faith is not about accomplishing goals or making the perfect decision. It is about having a life-changing encounter with the God of Abraham, Isaac, and Jacob—the Living God. As coaches we dedicate our life to Jesus Christ, the timeless One, who teaches us how to number our days and how to spend them in ways that work out for our greater good and His highest glory. That is the bedrock we stand upon whenever we coach.

In summary, keep in mind that when it comes to change and transformation, people must deny their old life and overcome personal habits of complacency and comfort. Once they've discovered they need to change and are motivated to be transformed by retaining you as a coach, it signals a *need* matched with a *desire* to change. Both must be present for success to be possible. Many people may need to change but are missing the desire to do it.

The role of the coach is to assist in establishing expectations so that the trainee can actualize the result they want or expect. To change, the trainee must be intentional. They will need to have a specific vision for their future, develop a plan of action, and have the ability to assess their personal progress.

Intentionality is vital when it comes to leading and coaching others. Human behavior is quite predictable in many areas, especially when it comes to changing one's behavior, or transformation. The apostle Paul tells us in Romans 12:2: not to conform *"to the pattern of this world, but be transformed by the renewing of your mind."* Taking action is a decision on the part of the trainee. They must act intentionally.

CHAPTER 7

Expectations and Results

Following Up and Moving Forward

Coaches can learn a lot from project managers and corporate executives because these people ensure a healthy organization and bottom line through successful project management skills. Project managers must consistently keep track of their project milestones—tasks and deliverables that must be completed by assigned dates and times.

In the same way, coaches assist trainees in understanding how to follow-up with their personal progress to keep them moving forward while accomplishing milestones or markers of success. An important part of realizing their goals is evaluating the progress that has been made and making plans for moving forward. Setting a SMART Goal includes being time specific. When the length of time they've set has come to an end, they need to review and evaluate their progress.

If the goal is one that will take a long time to accomplish, they may choose to set specific intervals to review and evaluate their progress (e.g. every thirty days or quarterly). Whatever the time period, there must be an agreed-upon "deadline." This is part of accountability. If circumstances have changed or the process has uncovered additional action steps that will be necessary for successful completion of a goal, this is the time for the coach and trainee to negotiate and revise the plan and pave the way for successfully reaching the revised goal.

Some questions to ask the person you are coaching:

- Are you on track to reach your goal in the timeframe I originally set?
- Have there been obstacles you didn't anticipate?
- What life circumstances have affected your progress?
- Do you need to revise your initial goal or reevaluate how long it will take to reach it?
- If you have already reached your goal, what is the next goal that will move you along in realizing your life vision?

Are *You* Ready?

Many people are interested in becoming a coach and believe it is beneficial. But interest and conviction alone do not make a good coach. A good coach is someone who knows what they're doing. Coaching is equipping others to live their fullest life (John 10:10b). SMART Goals can be a helpful tool to enable mature transformation, and it can also be used to *equip* people in developing life skills and in equipping them to help others do the same. Coaches cover a wide range of issues dealing with various growth areas for purposeful living.

Keep in mind that while some personality styles thrive on details and structure, others thrive on spontaneity and freedom. Form and freedom can complement each other and coexist beautifully when the coach and trainee recognize and embrace their differences.

-For Contemplation-

What are some ways you can equip those you coach (as well as yourself) for success?

Accountability is a plan for setting aside one-on-one time with a trainee—virtual or in person. A good coach will implement a "teach not tell" approach to coaching. Accountability is not telling people what to do; rather, it involves holding them accountable to think for themselves.

Consider coaching baseball as an example. If you coached a player in baseball, you might teach him to refine his stance, grip, and swing, but you do not hit the ball for him. Coaching is not doing for others what they can and must do themselves. Accountability is a way to encourage the person being coached to begin using valuable skills and practices right away, helping them to move from planning to implementation.

It is natural to want to cling to past accomplishments and dwell on previous successes, but setting new goals has the potential to shape who we are and who we are becoming. Setting new goals is an important discipline of the heart and mind. SMART Goals are an effective way to move into an entirely new vision of what God desires to bring about through us.

It can be helpful, too, if the people who want change are willing to state publicly what they plan to do and indicate who will hold them accountable. Public awareness and peer pressure are great motivators. It helps, as well, if the person who wants to change surrounds himself or herself with people who are encouraging and motivated to be achievers.

Predictability means setting clear expectations for yourself and the person you are coaching and meeting those obligations.

Planning helps both coach and trainee overcome obstacles in order to achieve desired results. Proper planning focuses attention on the things that truly matter. It is important to have intrinsic motivation, an attitude that says, "I know there may be many obstacles and problems, but I also have enough passion and power to make great choices to bring about change." This is the opposite of what psychology calls *learned helplessness,* which is doing something only because you are forced to do so because of a lack of planning (extrinsic motivation). Wise planning can help the trainee better serve those within their spheres of influence and also helps the coach in managing their time, energy, and resources more efficiently.

Proper planning helps trainees steward their resources and time more efficiently and effectively. This is different than the kind of boasting about tomorrow that James describes: *"Now listen, you who say, 'Today or tomorrow we will go to this or that city, spend a year there, carry on business and make money.' Why, you do not even know what will happen tomorrow. What is your life? You are a mist that appears for a little while and then vanishes. Instead, you ought to say, 'If it is the Lord's will, we will live and do this or that'"* (James 4:13-15 NIV).

Planning aids trainees in making space for God to work in their lives through the gift of His grace and through the mysterious work of the Holy Spirit to accomplish their tasks and achieve their goals. God has been faithfully at work before they ever show up on the scene. And when they look back at the results of their best planning and God's supernatural hand working with them, they can confidently say: "Only God could have done this."

Relevance is a critical component in coaching. Can the trainee see the real application of the coaching experience as worthwhile and useful in their life, either immediately or in the future? How can you help those you coach to see the relevance of your discussions and activities being worked out in their daily lives? SMART Goals is a skill set that amplifies the relevance and impact of coaching.

Competence can be gained by the trainee through a constant willingness to try new things and not being afraid to stretch him or herself and take risks. This means being open to learning from the mistakes they make. Self-confidence does not detract from full confidence in Christ and His Spirit working through them. Admitting that there are things they are not good at or do not know is a healthy part of coaching and a fundamental part of the growth process. It is impossible to move forward without making some mistakes and learning from them.

In fact, building and developing people's confidence is the best starting point for cultivating competence. Romans 15:1 says, *"We who are strong ought to bear with the failings of the weak and not to please ourselves"* (NIV). Jesus did this with Peter. Peter's name "Petros" meant rock—although the Apostle Peter was anything but a rock in the beginning. Yet, Jesus gave him the encouragement to live up to the potential of his name. Remember, everyone needs encouragement and confidence, and believing in and trusting those we coach brings out their best.

-For Contemplation-

What other questions come to mind that you can use to help your mentees with their personal goals?

Once they've achieved one goal, how can you keep the transformation process moving forward?

Relational Counseling

Everyone needs to talk to someone when they're experiencing challenges in their lives. Trainees will experience challenges in achieving personal goals and part of coaching is becoming a trusted friend they can talk to.

As you develop trust with your trainees, they will seek advice from you. At this point, you've developed a relationship with your trainee that allows them to trust you and believe in you as a good friend. It is not simply advice that you are providing; you encourage them to become more self-aware. At this point, you are engaging in relational counseling. Let's see what that looks like.

Since we all get asked for advice from time-to-time, how we give that advice is worth careful consideration. In this context, "Relational Counseling" includes almost anything that begins with an implied, "I think…" or "If I were you…" It is less formal than counseling, coaching, discipleship, or mentoring; it is simply advice. It works on the principle of friends talking to friends, informally, to offer support and a listening ear to those who ask for help, using Scripture as a guide.

It could be that during your interactions with trainees, you will be asked to give them some advice on "helping skills" that will equip them to support friends and neighbors who are working out how to deal with their own problems. In this way, you are helping them to grow in their personal lives, both emotionally and in other relationships. You will also want to provide them with an awareness of the nature of painful emotions in order to enable them to cope and respond constructively with others.

In relational counseling, we aim to engage a person in such a way that the person actually feels known, and then, in a joint enterprise, we (1) consider what God says (truth), recognizing that there is an interplay of many truths in Scripture, and (2) determine creative and suitable applications of what God says (opinion).

The apostle Paul makes a distinction in 1 Corinthians 7 between what God says and Paul's specific application of godly wisdom. We could say that one is truth and the other is opinion or advice. *"To the married I give this command [from the Lord]"* (v.10) in contrast with *"Now about virgins: I have no command from the Lord, but I give a judgment as one who by the Lord's mercy is trustworthy"* (v. 25). Of course, when Paul gives his opinion, we listen. But he knows he is speaking in a different way; he is giving advice.

Relational counseling requires caution. We do not want to offer a blanket statement without giving much thought to the particulars involved. The situation might end up confusing what is our own advice with what God says in His Word. Or maybe the person was not even seeking advice, but only wanted someone to listen. It is important to be sure we know what a person is asking for before we start talking. Maybe all the person wants is for someone to listen, not to "fix" something.

NOTE: *Coaching in Context* is built on the assumption that trainees are relatively free of psychological issues that could negatively impact or undermine coaching. If psychological problems do exist, they should be advised to receive counseling first before engaging a coach.

Learning from Mistakes

We all make mistakes and your trainees are no exception. Indeed, John C. Maxwell has an entire book on mistakes: *Failing Forward: Turning Mistakes into Stepping Stones for Success.* We all fail, but how we coach our trainees to respond to their failures is the difference between success and defeat. They cannot control the end results or fruit in their life, but they must take responsibility for addressing mistakes. As long as they live as a victim, they are doomed to fail.

It is the coach's trust and faith in God that allows them to draw from His resources. A good coach believes that God can use mistakes for good and trains the person they coach that reality. The epistle written by James begins, *"Consider it pure joy, my brothers and sisters, whenever you face trials of many kinds,"* (James 1:2 NIV). Having the mindset that trials are a normal, expected part of life, coupled with their faith, is a tremendous factor in their being able to cope with failures and disappointments. The role of the coach includes helping trainees learn how to find joy in trials and embrace failure and mistakes—to reframe them into something useful and beneficial.

Faith makes a significant difference in coaching. Having a dynamic faith allows the trainee to look past their mistakes and see the big picture of God's will becoming their own. If they desire what He desires, then they will need to focus on this dynamic faith, which is the unique image of God, living inside them as they dwell in His presence. Everyone makes mistakes but cannot shake God's redemptive purposes. When they learn to trust solely in Him rather than their own wisdom, their choices get easier.

We all know that the great King David was a brilliant strategist and leader. What makes him relatable is that he was also regularly begging for God's help. This passionate king knew from experience that depending on smartness alone could lead to some pretty lousy mistakes. But reliance on God's leadership through the illumination of the Holy Spirit would lead to wisdom. Paul, the apostle, also understood the importance of this, as seen in his letter to the Romans.

"The mind governed by the flesh is death, but the mind governed by the Spirit is life and peace" (Romans 8:6 NIV).

This may lead a person to wonder: If David and Paul lived like this, then how much *more* significance should *we* be placing on the Holy Spirit's guidance as we work with our trainees?

God never sheds light on our weaknesses to condemn or punish us. He does it so He can free us and break the cycle of our bondage to sin. When a trainee becomes frustrated with their circumstances, we should ask them, "What is God trying to refine and change in you?" God may be trying to work in our lives, too. Ultimately, we are all accountable to God for our own choices and decisions.

Our Ultimate Objective

Coaches diligently seek to set goals and objectives (and encourage those we coach to do the same), but everyone's worth is not ultimately tied to achieving goals and objectives. The underlying motivation for goal setting should be faithfulness and a commitment to stewardship over the resources and the responsibilities God has given to each of us. Christianity begins in the heart, and coaching in context encourages growth in the deeper heart issues of life—the spiritual and eternal well-being of those we coach. Our objective as a coach is to maximize our potential and expand our spheres of influence to honor God and make the best use of what He has wired us to do and be and to present that living example to our trainees.

There are times when a coach can help people improve their quality of life by simply helping them break free from their limitations and fears in order to enable them to find more balance in their lives. People sometimes come to you simply looking for help in some area of life that is out of alignment or lacking stability. There is power in being relational and not just informational. Coaching is much more than teaching; it is about relationships. This does not mean that coaching is absent of teaching—but simply that teaching is a smaller part of coaching. Relationships are at the core of coaching.

Projects, large or small, will be abandoned or successfully completed based on a word of encouragement—or the lack of one. Everyone needs friendships with inspiring people who will encourage us and urge us on; coaches provide that encouragement. All of us can benefit from having a coach, and each of us has the potential to be a coach. A coach positively impacts the lives and goals of the people they coach.

Everyone runs into the proverbial wall—blocked by what seems like an impassable barrier. For some individuals, it is easier to imagine failure than it is to imagine success. But sometimes reality will jar us awake and get us moving regardless of what we've imagined. Like the reality of knowing that God has already provided everything we need to accomplish His plan for our lives.

Allow me to illustrate my point with a story from a cruise my wife, Jacquie, and I took in Alaska and a tour of a dog-training kennel run by a musher named Matt, who ran his first Iditarod race in 2012.

The Iditarod is an epic dogsled race, held in early March, led by a driver (musher), with a team of dogs that covers over 1,000 miles of the roughest terrain in the world: jagged mountain ranges, dense forests, frozen rivers, and miles of desolate territory. This amazing race begins in Anchorage and ends in Nome on the Bering Sea coast.

No other extreme sport competition can compare! The race involves racing through blizzards causing whiteout conditions, sub-zero temperatures and gale-force winds, which can cause the wind chill to reach –100°F below zero and cause a complete loss of visibility, the hazards of overflow (slick ice from newly frozen water), long hours of darkness, and treacherous climbs over a grueling eight- to fifteen-day period. That is the Iditarod.

Matt explained that mushers and their dogs need more than a ton of supplies, which cannot be carried on the journey. Food and necessary provisions are taken along initially, but special containers are stored at designated stops along the way. As a musher, Matt eats and sleeps with his dogs. He massages the dog's sore muscles and tired feet, and he always carries an extra set of booties for each dog to accommodate their weather and terrain needs.

He told us that raising these dogs and knowing each one helps to identify their needs and care for them along the way. Caring properly for the dogs is the key to finishing the race well. He shared how important it is to KNOW that necessary supplies will be available along the way in order for him and his team to remain healthy and finish the race. If such detailed care is undertaken for a dog race, how much more care must God have already taken to put everything in place for His children, who are running a much more important race?

In many ways and in varying degrees throughout our lives, we sometimes find ourselves in a desperate struggle to survive. Perhaps our circumstances are not as hazardous as the Iditarod, but they can be just as challenging. Sometimes along the way, even when things are going well, we may feel like it is only a matter of time before we confront obstacles that will burden us with a sense of defeat. We may also be consumed by worry that something along the way will go awry.

But by God's grace, we see that His Word says, *"And God is able to bless you abundantly, so that in all things at all times, having all that you need, you will abound in every good work"* (2 Corinthians 9:8). Granted, the enemy of our soul, Satan, will point out how these words run counter to our experience when the winds are blowing furiously. Yes, the enemy is at war against our souls—but not just when the winds are blowing furiously—he is constantly at work trying to get us to drop out of the race we are running. And to souls weary of running, Jesus says, *"Come to me, all you who are weary and burdened, and I will give you rest"* (Matthew 11:28).

By the living Word of God we push onward. True to His promises, God has placed a constellation of mentors and coaches along the way to keep me in the race just when I need them. At the start, Christopher McCluskey was a prime encourager on my journey through formal training and growth as a coach trainer. At the next stop along the way, God provided someone who greatly influenced my thinking on coaching, Greg Campbell. Many of my perspectives about coaching were shaped by the Ultimate Leadership Workshops with facilitators Dr. John Townsend and Dr. Henry Cloud. And throughout it all, God has brought into my life people who have shaped me, encouraged me, and supported the development of this book—*Coaching in Context*.

People often tend to focus on the difficult circumstances that arise as they pursue their extreme goals. But goal setting does not guarantee success; faithfully running the race that He has placed before us does. As the missionary Jim Elliot said, "He is no fool who gives what he cannot keep to gain what he cannot lose."

There is never failure when we run our race well and leave the outcome of the race in God's hand. I have found that though others may break their commitments, God keeps His. *"And my God will meet all your needs according to the riches of his glory in Christ Jesus"* (Philippians 4:19). No matter what happens and regardless of what we've done or how far we've strayed off course, God never leaves us. Our only hope for finishing the race is found through the grace of God by faith in Jesus Christ!

Conclusion

At this point, I trust you have made some observations and decisions regarding your calling or role as a coach of others. Hopefully, you can relate to these four biblically supported statements that summarize the value of the *Coaching in Context* approach:

Four Reasons to Be a Coach

1. *You have a greater opportunity to use your spiritual gifts.* At the moment of your conversion, the Holy Spirit came to live inside you (1 Corinthians 6:19 NIV). When He did, He brought along the spiritual gift(s) that He sovereignly chose for you to possess for the blessing of the Church (1 Corinthians 12:7, 11). As we use our gifts, we are being good stewards of the manifold grace of God (1 Peter 4:10).

2. *You demonstrate your commitment to a spiritual family.* It shows that you want to be more than a bystander, that you want to be involved in ministry in a more significant way. This involves being fruitful as a servant. It shows that Jesus is our sole authority, our guiding light, and our unerring compass. *"For me to live is Christ"* (Philippians 1:21).

3. *You make yourself available to be part of the wisdom of a multitude of counselors.* God desires for us to develop relationships of accountability with other Christians. According to (Proverbs 11:14b), *"In the abundance of counselors there is victory."*

4. *You experience the joy of serving others.* God has made us "a new creation" in Christ Jesus (2 Corinthians 5:17) for the purpose of bringing glory to Him by bearing fruit (Ephesians 2:10; John 15:2). The fruit of the Spirit is primarily manifested in our relationships with others (Galatians 5:22-23). Believers are to follow the example of Christ, the Master Servant (John 13:15).

Never Stop Growing

A good coach will seek to develop a mindset of continual training and improvement by reading and reflecting on their experiences. Moreover, a good coach will recognize the need for seeking feedback from others, because we all need someone to turn to for listening and counseling. Transformation manifests itself differently in different people. In some cases, it may be a defining moment deeply embossed in memory, and for others, a deepening of faith over time that cannot be defined by one single event. No matter how widely our experiences differ, God's gift of salvation by His grace comes with the knowledge of our being called out of darkness into God's marvelous light (1 Peter 2:9).

God's mission includes restoring all aspects of our humanity and helping us navigate life and grow in Christlikeness. His ability to help us is regulated by how closely we abide in Jesus Christ and how well we understand Him and know ourselves. From there we can pursue knowing others, embrace the lifelong process of transformation, navigate through the various trials of life, and teach others.

Think about all your relationships. Know that God can bring change, health, and growth to each one, but He needs to start with us. If your goal is to coach other leaders and believers into better health, the greatest gift you can give them is a healthy you. Grow, learn, and make an impact within your spheres of influence by first bringing Him into every area of your life.

Most people simply stop investing time in their own growth process once they finish their formal education. To continue growing, you need to be proactive. Seminars, books, courses, and other venues help, but much of this learning remains only in our heads. You need to have the courage to become someone who is growing in all areas. One area of personal growth that we should nurture is our faith in God; remember, it is our faith that pleases God (Hebrews 11:6).

Here are a few tips for starting this process:

1. Seek to understand your own limitations by being aware of your emotions, wounds, etc. (Psalm 139:23).
2. Look for patterns and themes that reveal where you are most vulnerable (Psalm 139:24).
3. A state of continuous learning must be on purpose. So, develop a culture of continuous growth by making your own learning, growth, and development a priority (Psalm 119:105). Do not assume that you will automatically grow.
4. Make a list of skills or behaviors you want to improve. Then, pick one to work on, find a method to refine this ability, and practice those behaviors regularly. Doing so will lead to success (Psalm 1:1-3; Hebrews 13:21-22). John Maxwell often says, "Wisdom doesn't always come with age, sometimes age comes alone."

As for the continual growth of those you coach, keep in mind that *Coaching in Context* is not intended to be a substitute for the ongoing discipleship that all believers ought to participate in within the body of Christ. At various seasons in our lives, we could all benefit from the help of a coach, but this should not replace discipleship as God's long-term plan for our spiritual growth.

A profound and meaningful context for our growth and transformation in Christ is within the Church, and most specifically, in a small group. Regular participation in a small group allows us to grow in a safe Christian community that allows us to know others and become known by them in healthy ways. Small groups also provide regular opportunities to give and receive ministry as group members encounter the challenges of day-to-day life. God never intended for us to live life alone and isolated from others.

Bringing It All Together

We live in a culture that is obsessed with self-improvement and specialized training. It is easy to feel the need for improvement and training in various areas of our lives. Coaching, mentoring, and discipleship can all help us improve how we live, work, and relate. But we will never have perfect relationships in life, because sin separates us from God and from each other. Consequently, much in this coaching manual has been devoted to the power of emotional connection. Most leaders want to be more efficient and effective, but many do not understand that becoming an effective leader starts with connection—with relationship.

The emphasis is not on getting results as a coach, but to honor God by being the best we can be with the gifts and abilities He has given to us. *Coaching in Context* is a tool designed to give you some guidance in coaching. Its goal is to empower you to coach in the best way for your specific spheres of influence and talents. It is a resource that is designed to come along side you and partner with you to equip and encourage *those you coach*. We leave the results with God as we act upon His two great commandments as our guide (Matthew 22:37-39).

As a coach, you are helping individuals to embrace and declare something that the individual is trusting to be a reality—before it occurs. How is this so? It happens because we help them to dream big dreams, to set goals, and to practice the means to reach those goals. We also help them to set time markers for progress and to celebrate milestone achievements. Celebration is an effective coaching tool that encourages and builds confidence, gratitude, and joy.

At the same time, we are always aware that no one can know what the future holds with any degree of certainty. What we can know is that God always keeps His promises. So our vision and mission is shaped by God's faithfulness and our trust in Him and His promises.

In summary, *Coaching in Context* is not simply a mechanism for "fixing" people's lives, for helping people "improve" or become more effective in life. The goal is not satisfying our desire to handle life with greater confidence and competence. It is much more than mere self-improvement or self-help. The point is strengthening our connection and relationship with God and with people. We need to grow in Him and through Him, learning how to better love, encourage, serve, empower, and listen. Though this manual contains specific tools for growth, connection, and transformation, the ultimate goal and purpose of *Coaching in Context* is simply a more abundant life. Such a life is possible only through dynamic relationship with God and with our neighbors.

Appendix A

Biographical Reflection and Assessment

These sample questions can be used for your own reflection. Hopefully, through the process of questioning and responding, you will learn more about yourself and obtain a broader perspective of your experiences and background. The more thoughtful the responses, the more likely you will experience richer and more valuable coaching sessions.

Personal/Family:

1. How would you describe your childhood? Relationships with parents? Siblings? Other relatives? Friends?
2. How would you describe your current family/home life? Relationships with spouse, parents, children, significant others, and friends?
3. In a few succinct points, how would you describe yourself?
4. How would your friends and family describe you?
5. How would people you minister to describe you?
6. To what extent would you say you have a balanced life?

Occupational/Vocational

1. Describe your current work responsibilities.
2. In what ways do you consider your current job as a ministry or a way to serve God and His people?
3. If there was one thing you could change about where you work, what would you change?

Spiritual Life and Leadership

1. What spiritual gifts has God given you, and how are you using them? How have these gifts been confirmed, and how do you see their continued use?
2. Do you see yourself fulfilling your calling as a Christian? What additional opportunities for growth and learning exist?
3. How do you define success for yourself, and how will you know you are successful?
4. What motivates you?
5. List three of your most significant leadership strengths 1) from your point of view, and 2) from the viewpoint of others.
6. List three of your most significant leadership development needs 1) from your point of view, and 2) from the viewpoint of others.
7. Why do people follow your leadership?
8. Describe your strengths and development needs as an effective team member or team player.

Emotional Intelligence

1. What emotions are easy for you to express?
2. What emotions are difficult for you to express?
3. What emotions are hard for you to control?

Goals and Outcomes

1. In what ways do you hope to grow spiritually?
2. Where do you see yourself five years from now? What are the next steps in each important area of your life?

Appendix B

Identifying Your Personal Goals

It is your passion that brings vision to life. Goals are important, but people commit to causes (your vision), not to goals. You will want to align your goals and actions with your vision. Remember, your goals are intended to help you attend to the present and prepare you for the future. The concept of SMART Goals plans the path for success by helping you to monitor your progress in seeing your vision become a reality. Begin by clearly stating your goal in one short sentence.

My goal is to:

_____,

so that: _____

(this answers why the goal is important).

Now, ask yourself, is your goal:

Specific?	YES []	NO []
Measurable?	YES []	NO []
Attainable?	YES []	NO []
Related to your vision?	YES []	NO []
Time framed?	YES []	NO []

My plan of action:

The steps I am going to take to stay on track in accomplishing my goal are:

1. _____

2. _____

3. _____

Finding my starting point:

Even after we set goals and outline steps, we need to identify the actual starting place for working toward the goal. For example, if you decide that the primary resource you need to get started is more time in your schedule, identify an activity or responsibility you can eliminate or delegate to someone else. Is rearranging your schedule an option? Is there a piece of equipment you can acquire to make your work more efficient? As trivial as it may sound, this may be just the thing to fuel your motivation toward realizing your goal.

What can you identify as your first step toward realizing your goal?

_____

My plan for keeping myself accountable during the process:
My accountability partner: _____
Other ways I can keep myself accountable: _____

Potential obstacles are: *Ways to overcome the obstacles:*

1. _____   1. _____

2. _____   2. _____

3. _____   3. _____

Celebrate:

I will reward myself for accomplishing my goal by:

_____

_____

_____

Appendix C

Having a Plan

The questions in this section are designed to help you define the structure of goal setting, both for you and your trainees. The concepts here are easily adapted to fit individuals and their specific goal-setting needs.

1. What is the overall structure and content of your coaching plan?

2. Is your plan customized to the unique growth process of the individual you are working with?

3. What is included in your model that will help those you train to live out the mandate: to equip (disciple, prepare, train) the saints for the work of the ministry for the building up of the body of Christ? (Ephesians 4:11-12).

4. What will prayerfully happen as a result of your training? What are your trainees equipped to do?

5. If you had only four years left with no one to replace you, how would you spend your time over the next four years? How might this be different from your current use of time?

Note: As you and the person being coached work through the questions in Appendix B, make sure you spend time on OBSTACLES. Failure to acknowledge and include what is difficult will ensure that the goal will not be attained. Carefully considering the obstacles helps to clear the path and to keep you on track. Otherwise, you do not have a sense of the progress you are making.

Appendix D

Fifty Important Questions Coaches Should Ask

Here are fifty questions to stimulate clients to take action and achieve their personal goals, visions, and desires:

Personal

1. What personal development goals would you like to work on during our coaching relationship?
2. What is your passion in life?
3. What makes you laugh, cry, or become angry?
4. What is your preferred style of learning?
5. What are your top three strengths?
6. What are your key personal accomplishments?
7. What occupies most of your thought life?
8. How satisfied are you with your life?
9. How would you describe your life right now?
10. What do you like to do in your leisure time?

Interpersonal

1. How would you describe your current family life?
2. Whom do you admire most and why?
3. Who is your closest friend and why?

4. Describe your social life?
5. Whose company do you enjoy most and why?
6. What relationship has caused you the most pain?
7. What relationship do you most regret having and why?
8. What people do you find most threatening?
9. What people do you find most difficult?
10. Whose company do you least enjoy and why?

Intrapersonal

1. What background information is important for me to know about you?
2. Who were you closest to in your family growing up and why?
3. Are there areas of your past where you have unresolved wounds or hurts?
4. What difficult life experiences have had the greatest impact on you?
5. Have you taken temperament/personal strength assessments, and would you be willing to share the results?
6. What activities are most enjoyable to you?
7. When did you feel the greatest satisfaction and happiness in your life?
8. Who is easiest to talk to in your family?
9. Who are you closest to in your family now and why?
10. How would you describe your relationship with your parents/ siblings?

Career

1. What has been your greatest career challenge?
2. What are your career goals?
3. What has brought you the greatest joy in your work?
4. How would you rate your overall career satisfaction?

5. If you could do any kind of work regardless of ability or availability, what would you do?
6. How did you choose your career?
7. What encouraged you in your career choice?
8. Is anything holding you back in your career?
9. What do you enjoy most about your career?
10. What do you consider your life work?

Overcoming Obstacles

1. Have you ever held yourself back by fearing success? If so, how?
2. What are the values you are not willing to compromise?
3. What are your life's greatest roadblocks?
4. What is the biggest challenge you are facing right now?
5. What is the greatest obstacle you have had to overcome?
6. What people cause you the greatest difficulty at work?
7. If you could change just one thing about yourself, what would it be?
8. What about you would those who know you best most encourage you to change?
9. What attitudes are most troublesome to you?
10. What situations threaten you the most?

Appendix E

Verses for Servant Leadership

Note: The Greek words *diakonia* (service), and *diakonos* (servant: English: deacon), refers to people in leadership.

I commend to you our sister Phoebe, a deacon of the church in Cenchreae (Romans 16:1 NIV).

What then is Apollos? And what is Paul? Servants through whom you believed, even as the Lord gave opportunity to each one (1 Corinthians 3:5 NIV).

He has made us competent as ministers of a new covenant—not of the letter but of the Spirit; for the letter kills, but the Spirit gives life (2 Corinthians 3:6 NIV).

Rather, as servants of God we commend ourselves in every way: in great endurance; in troubles, hardships, and distresses (2 Corinthians 6:4 NIV).

Are they servants of Christ? (I am out of my mind to talk like this.) I am more. I have worked much harder, been in prison more frequently, been flogged more severely, and been exposed to death again and again (2 Corinthians 11:23 NIV).

You learned it from Epaphras, our dear fellow servant, who is a faithful minister of Christ on our behalf (Colossians 1:7 NIV).

If you continue in your faith, established and firm, and do not move from the hope held out in the gospel. This is the gospel that you heard and that has been proclaimed to every creature under heaven, and of which I, Paul, have become a servant (Colossians 1:23 NIV).

Tychicus will tell you all the news about me. He is a dear brother, a faithful minister and fellow servant in the Lord (Colossians 4:7 NIV).

Epaphras, who is one of you and a servant of Christ Jesus, sends greetings. He is always wrestling in prayer for you, that you may stand firm in all the will of God, mature and fully assured (Colossians 4:12 NIV).

Sources

The resources mentioned below have benefitted me over the years as I have been influenced and encouraged by a constellation of mentors and coaches. Christopher McCluskey, Greg Campbell, the Ultimate Leadership Workshops with facilitators Dr. John Townsend and Dr. Henry Cloud have greatly shaped and molded my understanding of coaching, and I share these resources in the hope they will benefit you as well.

Additional sources include:

Barna, George. *The Power of Vision*. (Regal Books, 2003).

Blackaby, Henry and Mel. *What's So Spiritual About Your Gifts?* (Sisters, OR: Multnomah, 2004).

Blackaby, Henry and Richard. *Spiritual Leadership: Moving People on to God's Agenda*. (Nashville: Broadman Holman, 2001).

Campbell, Greg and Dr. Steve Halliday. *The 5-2-1 Principle*. (San Bernardino: 2015).

Chesterton, G.K. *"What's Wrong with the World,* The collected works of GK Chesterton IV. (San Francisco: Ignatius Press, 1987).

Collins, Gary R. PH.D. *Christian Coaching, 2nd ed.: Helping Others Turn Potential into Reality.* (NavPress, 2014).

Covey, Stephen M. R. *The Speed of Trust: The One Thing That Changes Everything.* (New York: Free Press, 2006).

Craig, William Lane. ON GUARD: *Defending Your Faith with Reason and Precision.* (David C. Cook, 2010).

Engstrom, Ted W. and Ron Jenson. *The Making of a Mentor.* (Waynesboro, GA: Authentic Media [in partnership with World Vision], 2005).

Flaherty, James. *Coaching: Evoking Excellence in Others*, 2nd ed. (Oxford: Butterworth-Heinemann, 2005).

Goldsmith, Marshall and Mark Reiter. *Triggers: Creating Behavior That Lasts—Becoming the Person You Want to Be.* (New York: Crown Business, 2015).

Harkavy, Daniel S. *Becoming a Coaching Leader: The Proven System for Building Your Own Team of Champions.* (Thomas Nelson, 2010).

Jensen, Ron. *Make a Life, Not Just a Living.* (Thomas Nelson Publishers, 1995).

Lewis, C.S. *The Weight of Glory.* (New York: Macmillan, 1949).

Lewis, C. S. *Mere Christianity.* (HarperOne, 2012).

London, H.B. and Neil B. Wiseman. *Pastors at Greater Risk.* (Regal Books, 2003).

Lyons, Kay. As quoted by "Quotable Quotes" accessed December 9, 2018, Good Reads.

Maxwell, John C. *15 Invaluable Laws of Growth: Live Them and Reach Your Potential.* (Center Street, 2012).

Ross, David and Rick Blackmon. *"Soul Care for Servants"* workshop reported the results of their Fuller Institute of Church Growth research study in 1991 and other surveys in 2005 and 2006; Focus on the Family 2009 survey of 2,000 pastors.

Sala, Dr. Harold J. *Getting Acquainted With the Holy Spirit.* (OMF literature Inc., 2017).

Sinek, Simon. *Start With Why: How Great Leaders Inspire Everyone To Take Action.* (New York: Penguin Group, 2011).

Stoltzfus, Tony. *Leadership Coaching: The Disciplines, Skills, and Heart of a Coach.* (Longwood, FL: Xulon, 2005).

Stoltzfus, Tony. *Coaching Questions: A Coach's Guide to Powerful Asking Skills.* (Coach 22 Bookstore LLC, 2008).

Thurman, Dr. Chris. *The Lies We Believe about God: Knowing God for Who He Really Is.* (Thomas Nelson, 2003).

Townsend, Dr. John. *Leadership Beyond Reason.* (Thomas Nelson, 2009).

Webb, Keith E. *The COACH Model for Christian Leaders: Powerful Leadership Skills to Solve Problems, Reach Goals, and Develop Others.* (Active Results, 2013).

White, Daniel. *Coaching Leaders: Guiding People Who Guide Others.* (San Francisco: Jossey-Bass, 2005).

Willard, Dallas. *Hearing God.* (InterVarsity Press, 2012).

Willard, Dallas. *Knowing Christ Today.* (HarperOne, 2009).

Willard, Dallas. *Renovation of The Heart.* (NavPress, 2002).

Zacharias, Ravi and Vince Vitale. *Jesus Among Secular Gods: The Countercultural Claims of Christ.* (Faith Words, Hachette Book Group, 2017).

About the Author

Dr. Wil Chevalier is the co-founder and executive director of LifeBranch Institute International, a non-profit corporation dedicated to Christian leadership development and marriage enrichment. He holds an MA from BIOLA University, an MDiv from Asian Theological Seminary, and a DMin from Trinity Seminary. Wil also did postgraduate work at the Asia Graduate School of Theology, Manila. Wil was a middle manager for Pacific Telephone and served as a shareowner-relations manager for AT&T. Upon leaving Pacific Telephone, Wil became the Asian director of Guidelines, Inc., a mission agency dedicated to reaching the family through print and broadcast media.

Wil is a certified mediator, trained through Dispute Resolution Services (DRS), a non-profit corporation of the Los Angeles Bar Association. He received training through the Barristers Domestic Violence Project (L.A. Bar Assoc.), the Victim-Offender Reconciliation Program Cross Training of Orange County and was a member of the Orange County Task Force for Promise Keepers' Ethnic and Denominational Reconciliation (1995-1997).

Wil and his wife, Jacquie, work as a team at LifeBranch conferences and leadership development seminars. For more than 30 years, they have conducted trainings in the areas of conflict management, communication, and marriage/family issues. They are certified with the IBCC (International Board of Christian Counselors) as Crisis Response Specialists through CISM, International Critical

Incident Stress Foundation, Inc. They are also members of the American Association of Christian Counselors, and the International Press Association.

Wil and Jacquie have also spoken at conferences for the American Association of Christian Counselors, the Christian Management Association, Smart Marriages, and the Urban Congress on the Family. They travel widely, speaking and teaching throughout the United States, Asia, Africa, New Zealand, Cuba, Mexico, Central America, Haiti, and Ukraine. The Chevaliers have authored several books, including *The Agony & Ecstasy of Intimacy, More Than Love, Marriage Beyond the Garden, Parenting the Coming Generation,* and *Embracing the Mystery of Love and Marriage* Additionally, Wil wrote *Shaking the Family Tree* and recorded three music albums that reflect the messages of love and reconciliation.

LifeBranch Institute, Inc.
P.O. Box 8097, Laguna Hills, CA 92654
www.lifebranch.com

Printed in the United States
By Bookmasters